Nationwide
Acclaim for

STAYING
HOME

The authors provide a wealth of information . . . . **A must for all mothers**
who are (or want to be) at home with their children.
— *Publishers Weekly*

Women are blazing new trails in balancing work and family. Very different
from the at-home mothers of the fifties, these women consciously
"sequence," moving in and out of the workplace as their needs and their
families' needs change. Our members tell us that **Staying Home has
become their road map** as they make that journey.
— Joanne Brundage, Executive Director, Mothers & More

A friendly guidebook for transitioning from the office to home. **Staying
Home** helps mothers navigate through their new circumstances and find
creative strategies for making their at-home career work for them.
— *At-Home Mother*

Highly recommended reading for all mothers in the process of choosing
whether or not to be full-time homemakers and parents.
— *The Midwest Book Review*

Making the decision to stay home with my two children after a 12-year
demanding, successful career that I loved was very difficult for me. It was
a decision I never expected to make. I started to read **Staying Home** and
I couldn't put it down. **Staying Home laid out the challenges and the
benefits**, and made me see that this was **a positive choice** I could move
towards with my self-respect and identity fully intact!
— Laurie Tennant, Orinda, CA

I was trying to decide whether or not to go back to work, and this book was exactly what I needed to read. **Staying Home put into words the feelings that I had in my heart** . . . . It helped me to put things into perspective and . . . take seriously my role as a mother at home. I've recommended this book to dozens of other new mothers. And every time I'm feeling a bit under-appreciated in my role and need a boost, **I pick up the book again and feel refreshed and renewed** in my decision.
— Gin Shaw, Atlanta, GA

Staying Home is a phenomenal resource for women considering at-home mothering. It addresses issues of living on one income, relationships between friends, relatives, and the "outside" world, and how to reaffirm your decision and be happy with yourself. **The authors have great insight into women and their feelings** . . . .
— Cindy Schival, Alpharetta, GA

Thanks for the good read! I first found **Staying Home** in our county library when I was disconsolately looking for some—any—material on moms who choose to be home. I was thrilled to find the book and it really made me feel better about my choice. The book really made me realize there were **other options besides working full-time**.
— Mary Williams, via e-mail

Issues of self-esteem and identity regarding stay-at-home parenting are not gender-specific. While trading in my globe-trotting, professional ways for life as 'Mr. Mom' was certainly the best thing I've ever done, it was not without far-reaching consequences for me in ways I never would have imagined. **Staying Home resonated loudly for me. I'll be giving this book to a few friends in the next several months**.
— Scott Paton, Mom.com

Includes Information on National Mothers' Organizations

Staying Home: A Growing Trend

- U.S. Census Bureau data indicate that 60.2% of the 26.4 million married-couple families with children below age 18 have a non-employed mother or a mother employed part-time, and that American women average 11.5 years out of the paid labor force.[1]

- "A rising proportion of young women appear to be choosing motherhood over career," notes Jane Bryant Quinn in *Newsweek*. "It's one of prosperity's side effects. When couples can manage on just one income (or one and a half), they lean toward part-time work or staying home full time." [2]

- "The stay-at-home impulse started gathering steam in the 1980s, as growing ranks of professional women chose to go part-time or take extended leaves to devote more time to their families. . . . ," *The Wall Street Journal* reports. [3]

- "Today's under-35 women say they're ambitious, but they aim to have families first, careers later—and, even more than baby boomers, they consider motherhood 'the most important job in the world,'" according to the Update: Women research project . [4]

- A *Parents* magazine poll finds that 43% of 18,000 mothers surveyed say they would like to stay home (nearly twice as many mothers who felt that way in 1989), and 56% of women feel "it is better for the child if the mother does not work." [5]

- When asked what would make them happiest, 39% of the women participating in a women.com survey chose being an at-home mom; 47% chose working from home while caring for their baby. [6]

(1)Mothers at Home, www.mah.org; Mothers & More, www.mothersandmore.org (2) Jane Bryant Quinn, "Revisiting the Mommy Track," Newsweek, July 17, 2000, p. 44. (3) Nancy Ann Jeffrey, "The New Economy Family," The Wall Street Journal, September 8, 2000, p. W1. (4) "Now the Word is Balance," USA Weekend, May 9, 1999. (5)"Women & Work" poll and reader survey, Parents, May 1996 (6) Women.com online survey, April 27, 2000.

By the same authors

Darcie Sanders and Martha M. Bullen
Turn Your Talents Into Profits

Martha M. Bullen, co-editor
Tales From The Homefront

Staying Home
From Full-Time Professional to Full-Time Parent

Darcie Sanders and Martha M. Bullen

Spencer & Waters

Boulder, Colorado

TENTH PRINTING
2005

Copyright © 1992 by Darcie Sanders and Martha M. Bullen

Excerpt from *Ourselves and Our Children: A Book By and For
Parents* by The Boston Women's Health Book Collective.
Copyright © 1978 by The Boston Women's Health Book
Collective, Inc. Reprinted by permission
of Random House, Inc.

Library of Congress Cataloging-in-Publication Data

Sanders, Darcie
      Staying Home : from full-time professional to full-
time parent / Darcie Sanders and Martha M. Bullen. – 1st
ed.
      p. cm.
      Includes bibliographical references (p.).
      ISBN 0-967-03590-2
      1.   Motherhood – United States. 2. Work and
          family – United States. 3. Parenting – United
          States. I. Bullen, Martha M.

      HQ759.S19   1992
      306.874'3 – dc20   92-2839

Designed by Barbara Werden

Published by Spencer & Waters, Lyons, Colorado
http//:www.spencerandwaters.com

Printed in the United States of America

To our mothers, who stayed home for us

Contents

Contents

Preface

This book was written to help women, especially mothers with young children and those who are expecting or hoping to be mothers someday, understand why so many women are choosing to interrupt their careers to devote themselves to raising their children. You'll find a new job description and career path to guide you through the most personally significant career change of your life: motherhood.

You've probably noticed that more and more of the women you know are embracing full-time motherhood after their children are born. This is a growing trend across the country that has been building over the past several years. Unfortunately, motherhood is still an invisible profession in the eyes of society and the media. Although nearly half of all mothers of preschool children stay home with their children, the image of the supermom is still all-too-prevalent whenever we pick up a newspaper or watch television.

Motherhood is a career that has its own responsibilities, rewards, and challenges. It offers more opportunities for fulfillment and freedom than most other jobs in the working world. Yet many mothers still feel as though they are considered "less equal" than others who work for pay.

In fact, motherhood may be the most controversial career you can have these days. This may sound like an exaggeration, but women who make this choice are often greeted with surprise, disapproval, and a lack of understanding from their friends, family, and coworkers.

We've heard from hundreds of mothers that when they announced their intention to leave their jobs, they were confronted with comments such as "Don't resign, you'll ruin your life"; "You're crazy to quit your job and throw your career away"; "I'm sure your brain will turn to mush, and you'll be back at work before you know it." These reactions make a difficult decision even more painful and can make a new mother feel as though her friends have abandoned her.

Because a mother who would like to stay home and raise her children too often finds little support for her decision, many women hesitate to make this choice. "What *do* at-home mothers do all day?" they wonder. "Will I be wasting my education and the career skills I've learned over the past several years? Will my family and friends respect my choice? How can I manage without my own paycheck?"

We hope to answer these questions in this book and to help you make an informed decision about whether you're ready to change from a career woman to a career mother. Since women who have been in the work force can face a difficult transition in adjusting to life at home, we also offer ways to help you apply your professional skills at home and to make the most of your mothering years.

Acknowledgments

We gratefully acknowledge the contributions of the following people. This book could not have been written without their help and encouragement. Our thanks to:

The members of FEMALE, Mothers at Home, and the hundreds of women and men who shared their experiences with eloquence and honesty through our survey and personal interviews. We continue to be profoundly moved by their insights.

Martha's father, Bruce A. Mahon, who went far above and beyond the call of duty when he developed the database for our survey and performed the tedious task of data entry and analysis. We are grateful for his expertise in uncovering the meaning behind the survey results.

Our children, Claire, Stuart, and J.T., who were constantly teaching us more about at-home motherhood throughout the entire writing process, even during those times when we were unwilling students.

This book would not have been possible without the guidance and enthusiasm of Ann Cocks, Maryann Wegloski Cooke, Pat Ensworth, Laurie Koblesky, Paul A. Mahon, Michael McDonnell, Charlotte Schneider, John Wasik, and Kathleen Wasik.

Thanks also to our agents and editors — Eileen Fallon, Barbara

Acknowledgments

Lowenstein, Ellen Denison, Becky MacDougall, and Kit Ward — who had faith in the project, and whose intelligence and sensitivity undeniably improved the work.

And, of course, special thanks to Martin Bullen and Lenny Karpel, who in innumerable ways helped to father this book.

Introduction

Mothers at Home: The New Trendsetters

Even though full-time mothers are often treated as dinosaurs on the verge of extinction, there are far more at-home mothers than most people think. Millions of American women work at home caring for their young children. The national Mothers at Home support organization reported that the *majority* of preschool children are cared for by their own parents: "54% have a mother at home, 7% have 'tag team' parents, and 4% accompany their mothers to work or are cared for by mothers who earn income at home."[1]

Never before in history have so many women who worked outside the home faced the prospect of returning to the home — whether it be for three months, three years, or permanently. Competent, accomplished professional women, some with a decade of advanced schooling and another decade of job experience, are giving up their on-the-job identities for a new one: at-home mom.

This life-style change is not limited to professional women. There are some indications that family values are becoming more important in our society after the money-grubbing excesses of the 1980s. In May 1991 *USA Today* reported what it considered "a stunning trend": for the first time since the Labor Department began keeping statistics in 1948, the percentage of women in the work force had dropped. Government analysts attributed this drop primarily to women who are choosing to stay home with their children. *USA Today* noted, "Anecdotal evidence suggests a shift in values is taking place, at least among women who can afford to quit work."[2]

At-home mothers aren't the only ones who are questioning our society's relentless pursuit of work and its neglect of family values. Many pollsters are finding that working men and women across the country would also prefer to have one parent at home if they could afford it. Here are just a few examples:

- A *Self* magazine survey of women aged eighteen to forty-nine found that nearly three-quarters said they were more concerned with balancing work and family than with being "supersuccessful," and 75 percent placed family over work when asked to choose between the two.[3]
- A *Washington Post/ABC News* poll found that eight out of ten parents with children under age fourteen believe it is best for children to be cared for by parents at home. [4]
- A *USA Today* survey found that 73 percent of all two-parent families would have one parent stay home with children "if money were not an issue." [5]
- The Gallup Poll reported that among all adults, 63 percent "believe that the "ideal family situation for children" is where "the father has a job and the mother stays home and cares for the children," [6]
- A *Los Angeles Times* survey of 1,000 families discovered that 57 percent of fathers and 55 percent of mothers feel guilty about spending too little time with their children. In addition, seventy-nine percent of the mothers and 39 percent of the fathers polled said that they would quit their jobs if they could to stay home with their kids.[7]
- A Cornell University study found that two-thirds of all mothers who work full-time would prefer to work fewer hours and devote more time to their families.[8]

- *Public Opinion* magazine reported that 88 percent of the mothers polled who worked outside the home either full-time or part-time agreed with the following statement: "If I could afford it, I would rather be home with my children."[9]

As these polls indicate, there is hope that attitudes about the relative importance of work and family are changing. One mother told us, "My quitting my job was a statement: my child comes first. Work will have a place in my life sometime, but it will never again dominate it."

Who Is Today's Mother at Home?

In researching this book, we surveyed more than 600 women across the country on all aspects of their lives as at-home mothers and conducted 40 in-depth personal interviews with men and women. The mothers we surveyed are similar in that they all share the decision to stay home with their children for a significant portion of time, but they also show a great deal of diversity in age, income, region, and professional background. Some of these women have six children, and some have one child. Some are continuing to work on a part-time or free-lance basis, while others have left the work force entirely for several years. Their personal experiences and heartfelt comments, as well as the statistics reported in the book, were taken from our four-page survey and personal interviews. (The survey and its results appear on pages 215–227.)

Throughout the book, we use our survey results to look beyond the stereotypes of the "June Cleaver" image of the at-home mother and give you the other side of the story.

We learned that today's mother at home is like her own mother in many ways. Many of the women we interviewed said that they saw their own mother as a positive role model in making the choice to stay home. Several women commented that they stayed home "because of my mother's example" and explained, "She was home with me, and I feel that's what you're supposed to do as a mother."

Full-time mothers these days experience the same rewards as mothers through the ages — the joys of watching their children grow and being there for all the important moments. They also experience many of the same frustrations — feeling unfulfilled at times and frustrated by the continual demands of children and endless household chores.

But modern at-home mothers differ from their predecessors in several important ways. They often spend several years establishing a career before taking some time off at home. They have gained valuable professional experience and made a name for themselves, which will be of great help when they are ready to return to the work force.

In addition, at-home mothers generally consider their time at home as only one stage of their lives. They want to be home with their young children, but they almost always plan to resume a paid career when their children are older. "Women now are definitely seeing this as a temporary part of their lives. That is totally different from how it was then," said Helena Lopata, a sociology professor who interviewed several hundred suburban homemakers in the 1950s and 1960s. She reported in her book *Occupation: Housewife* that 46 percent of the nearly 500 women she spoke to then had no intention of seeking a job in the future. Few of the mothers mentioned an identification with their careers, and one-third said that they had no career goals other than being a housewife. "Today, it is a different bag entirely," she noted.[10]

Today's at-home mothers also tend to be older and better educated than their mothers and grandmothers were when they stayed home with their children. They are less likely to feel stuck at home and are more inclined to get out of the house and actively search for support from other mothers.

Most important, mothers at home today have *chosen* to devote their time and talents to raising a family. Janet Hodge, a nurse therapist in private practice, raised three daughters in the 1960s and 1970s. When we asked her why she decided to stay home with her children, she replied, "I don't think I ever thought of anything else. I didn't think I had an option. I had been working as a nurse before my oldest daughter was born, but it never occurred to me to continue working." In some ways, that attitude made life easier for mothers then. While they may not always have been happy at home, they didn't experience the agony of wondering what path to choose, and they didn't face criticism when they did stay home.

All of the women in their twenties and thirties whom we interviewed said that they had thought long and hard about their options before deciding to make their children their top priority. Many of the mothers struggled with terrible doubts and conflicts before making their decision. A large number did return to the workplace after their child was born, and only after doing their best to juggle work and motherhood did they conclude that they couldn't handle both jobs as well as they wanted to. Others decided to come home after the birth of a second or third child.

As more and more professional women choose full-time motherhood, whether for a year or a decade, they have the opportunity to serve as role models and to show others that motherhood is a valid, important, and honorable career choice.

Making the Transition from Professional to Professional Parent

1

Motherhood: The Ultimate Full-Time Job

This is the greatest thing I've ever done in my life
by far — the most profound and most enriching.
Yes, you deal with a lot of adjustments, but
eventually raising your child at home is very deeply
satisfying.
— Laurie Koblesky, *free-lance writer and at-home
mother of two pre-schoolers*

"My name is Janet. Three months ago I gave up my full-time
position in the lab in order to stay home with our first child. I'm
delighted with my baby — couldn't love or enjoy her more — but
I'd be lying if I said I didn't miss the companionship and accomplishments I used to enjoy at work. Still, I'm pretty sure I'll stay at
home for a few more years, at least; this time is very precious, and
I don't want to miss my baby's childhood. Anyway, here's what
happened to me.

"Last week I went out to a barbecue given by some friends. I
was really looking forward to it, actually longing for an afternoon off
and some adult conversation. I was eager to talk about the latest
plays, politics, or anything other than bottles and bowel move-
ments.

"Oh, sure, I did have some misgivings. I was worried about
the qualifications of the baby-sitter (even though she was my own

mother), worried that my daughter might miss me, worried that she wouldn't miss me. I also felt awkward in clothes that did not fit as well as they used to and was embarrassed that I needed to use makeup — something I don't usually use — to cover the dark rings that had installed themselves under my eyes during countless four A.M. feedings.

"My husband, John, told me I looked great, and off we went. We knew most of the people at the barbecue, and there were many lively conversational groups to join, but no one asked me anything but 'How's the baby?' or 'What's happening on the soaps these days?' None of my old friends talked to me directly about being at home. It was as though I was out on probation, and they were all too polite to mention that I had been in jail and was no longer a contributing member of society. When the talk did turn to current events or gossip from the lab, the other people addressed their comments to John and skipped right over me. I wondered if, despite the weight I'd gained, I was becoming invisible.

"A small group of older women were in the kitchen preparing salads and talking about problems with Little League and the local school board, and even though I hate to cook and am many years away from being concerned with school politics, I felt as though maybe that was where I should be.

"The thought was so abhorrent to me that I wandered off and tried starting a conversation with a group of people I didn't know. I really thought I was doing fine, too, until someone asked me, 'And what do you do, Janet?'

"I went blank. I was absolutely unprepared for this question. I didn't like any of the possible answers.

"I told one man, 'I'm a mother at home,' and was greeted with, 'Oh, that's nice,' and the sight of his back as he wandered off to find someone more important to talk to. I tried using my former job title with the next person I talked to but felt bad about downplaying the importance of my new job as a mother — as if I was betraying my daughter. After a while, I just said, 'I work at home,' and tried to avoid any further questions. I did overhear another woman in her mid-thirties with a suspiciously familiar stain on the shoulder of her shirt say the same thing. I wondered, 'Is she really just a mother, too?' but was afraid to ask.

"We ended up leaving the barbecue early because I got such a bad headache. All the way home I was on the verge of tears but couldn't bring myself to express to John just how miserable I felt. I wondered, 'Why was that so painful? Who am I, now that I've left my job? Why can't a person who happens to be a mother be taken seriously — by others and herself?' "

Do you know a "Janet" — a friend, a coworker, a cousin, yourself? When people talk about balancing family and work life, does something in you cry out, "Half isn't enough?" Do you also wonder aloud, as one at-home mother did, "Who in her right mind would surrender an identity as a self-supporting professional in favor of diapers, drool and doldrums?"[1]

In many ways, Janet is a typical at-home mother: educated, liberated, dedicated, and frustrated. Yet despite their fears about not working outside the home, many women choose to stay home rather than deliver their children into the care of another.

As you can see from Janet's experience, this is not an easy choice to make. Certainly, there is no one right way to raise our children. Staying home is not an option for every family: single parents, couples who could not survive financially on one salary, and women who are committed to their careers and unwilling to leave the positions they've worked hard to achieve may be better off remaining in the workplace. It's important to take the time to think over your alternatives and to build the life that is best suited to you and your family, whatever that may be.

Twenty Benefits of Being an At-Home Mother

We decided to ask the hundreds of at-home mothers in our survey why they made the decision to stay home to raise their children. The following compelling reasons came up time and again. If you are confronting this issue in your own life, we hope this list of the benefits of at-home motherhood will help you in making a choice. If you are already a full-time mother, we hope this section will reaffirm your decision.

I'm the best one to raise my child; no one else can do it as well. As Maryann Wegloski Cooke, a former accountant who has been at home with her oldest son for three years, commented, "At the beginning, what children really need is to be loved, and no one else can do that as well as I can." Parents have a vested interest in their children's development, which makes them best qualified to care for them.

Cynthia Copeland Lewis puts it this way: "Every mother knows that much of what motivates her to cheerfully spend her mornings playing dress-up, teddy bear parade, and dinosaur puppet show is the deep emotional commitment she has to her child."[2]

I'm not missing my child's childhood. We heard this reason again and again. Going back to work full-time would mean just being with my child on evenings and weekends, many mothers told us, and that's not enough. These mothers don't want to miss their once-in-a-lifetime chance to spend the most important years of their children's lives with them. Having a difficult pregnancy or having a child after many years of trying also can convince a woman to stay home. Mary Clauss left her prestigious job as sales development manager for American Express to stay home with her infant son. She said, "I couldn't have children initially and had to go to an infertility specialist. We thought, why would we have spent so much time and money having a child and then pay someone else to raise him?"

I fell in love with my child. Some of the mothers we spoke to had made up their minds years before having a child that they would stay home. Others didn't decide until they first held their baby or when their maternity leave came to an end and leaving their child was too difficult. ArLynn Leiber Presser, a Chicago lawyer, talks about the difficulty in trying to continue her practice after her son was born: "It is easy to talk about combining kids and careers until you really do the mixing. The problem is not, as many of the young feminists I meet at the law school apparently believe, that some repressive male chauvinists are bent on keeping women in the home. The problem is that women care too much about their children to want to [hand them over] to someone else."[3]

I have a deeper relationship with my child because I am home. Most of the mothers we spoke to felt that their being home full-time allowed them to develop a deep, loving relationship with their children. Lucinda Michaelis, a speech pathologist, put it this way: "I was afraid if I went back to work too early, I wouldn't know my son and he wouldn't know me." Other women talked about the "relaxed rapport" they had together and the sense of security they were giving their children.

In the book *What's a Smart Woman Like You Doing at Home?* the founders of the Mothers at Home support group note, "It is ironic that a nation that has developed a veritable fetish of 'bonding' with an infant at birth advises us of the wisdom of leaving them as early as a tender six weeks of age. . . . There is no specific age when a child stops needing you."[4]

Raising my child is a job that really matters. Let's face it, we don't all have power jobs. Not every career is fulfilling and glamorous. In her book about motherhood, Mary Ann Cahill writes that contrary to popular belief, "a mother-at-home does not have to be stifled, bored, or unfulfilled. People can be stifled, bored, and unfulfilled in places and positions far from home."[5]

Numerous mothers told us that when they're feeling frustrated or regretting their lapsed careers, it helps them to remember that staying home is of great importance to their children. Being there with your children and encouraging their development also can be much more rewarding than shuffling papers in an office. One mother commented, "I don't feel unfulfilled not having an outside career; my work as a mother will make a difference forever."

We're raising our children with our values. Many of the mothers we interviewed told us that they decided to stay home to make sure their children will share their moral and religious values. Barbara Galli is married to a minister, and she and her husband agree that instilling values is one of the most important parts of a parent's job. She told us, "I wanted to be around to deal with situations where my values could be expressed and taught. I don't want to give that much authority to other people to raise my children."

Other mothers are particularly concerned with passing along their family's cultural traditions to their children. They're interested in creating and preserving their own family's unique traditions, whether they are ethnic or religious customs or just family outings and special holiday rituals.

I'm my child's first teacher. Many women choose to stay home to participate in their child's intellectual development. The first few years of life are crucial to a child's personality formation and world-view, and many mothers don't want to miss this teaching opportunity. Children can benefit from receiving much more individual attention at home than they will get in school or in a day-care center.

Several of the college graduates we interviewed said that they can't think of a better use of their education than helping their children grow, learn, and discover the world. One mother says, "Five years ago I stopped teaching math to seventh and eighth graders to become a mother. . . . [Now] I have a full-time teaching position at home."[6] Teaching young children can be an intellectual challenge, as you search the depths of your memory for the answers to your children's endless questions about the world around them.

We've heard from a surprisingly large number of mothers who've decided to take this one step further and provide home schooling for their children. They feel that they can do a better job of understanding their children's strengths and weaknesses and encouraging them to learn than the educational system can.

I don't have to worry about "quality time." Having unlimited time together with your children is an important benefit of being at home. Many women told us that it's wonderful not to feel rushed and that they can sit down with their children to talk or play without having to keep an eye on the clock. The women we surveyed were dubious about the concept of "quality time" and said they would choose "quantity time" any time. One mother notes, "I have my own definition of quality time for a child. Quality time is the exact moment your child needs you, not an hour at the end of the day that you set aside for your child."[7]

I'm not stressed out from working two full-time jobs. Jacqueline Steltz-Lenarsky previously worked as a research assistant for a child psychiatric clinic. She told us, "I had actually gotten a new job and had verbally accepted it, and then I decided I couldn't do it. I couldn't give one hundred percent to my job and my child. I saw how stressed out 'working women' were in trying to juggle work and home, and that influenced my decision."

Many at-home mothers wonder how women who are employed manage to fit in time for themselves and their husbands, not to mention time for personal interests and for sleep. They think that working and caring for their children would completely use up all of their time, patience, and energy. A recent survey confirmed that belief. It found that working women with children are more than twice as likely as working men with children to feel constant stress and to feel trapped by their daily routine.[8]

Other at-home mothers were surprised to find out that even though they enjoyed their jobs, after they returned to work they felt heartbroken and longed to be home with their children. Elissa Frederick Hardy, an ophthalmic surgical technologist who is now at home, told us, "As a working mother, I felt so torn apart a lot of the time. If I found myself absorbed and happy in my work, I would have a sharp pang wondering, 'How is my son right now?' "

I don't have to feel guilty or worry about how my child is cared for when I'm not there. About 3 percent of the mothers we spoke to said that they had planned to return to their jobs after their maternity leave but they either could not find child care they were comfortable with or they could not afford it. Many mothers said that day-care costs would have eaten up most of their salary, so it wasn't cost-effective for them to return to work. As Chris Golko notes, "As an elementary school teacher in a Chicago Catholic school, my returning to work and paying for daycare was a financial joke. By the time I would dress myself, contribute to my classroom needs and pay daycare, I would have owed money."[9] Others told us, "I didn't feel I could make day care work and feel good about it. That was not the kind of childhood I wanted my children to have."

Donna Malone decided to go from full-time work as a marketing research vice president to part-time work at home because "I really couldn't deal with the guilt anymore. I didn't want to spend any more time away from my daughter. When I worked full-time, every night she'd ask, 'Mom, is tomorrow a workday?' If I said yes, she'd start crying. If I said no, she'd start jumping up and down on the bed with joy. We went through that every night. Thank God that's never an issue anymore."

I'm my own boss and have the freedom to set my own schedule. "The best thing about being at home full-time is that you're in charge," says Gini Hartzmark. "I run my household and I control the kind of childhood my kids are going to have."[10] When you're a mother at home, you don't have to wear suits or pantyhose, fight rush-hour traffic, punch a clock, or take orders from your boss. You *are* the boss, perhaps for the first time in your professional career, and that can be a wonderful feeling.

Heidi L. Brennan, codirector of the Mothers at Home organization, told us that she loves the freedom that comes with at-home motherhood: "There's tremendous freedom — it's the most liberated you're ever going to be." Other mothers told us they enjoy "being on the slow track" for a few years and having time to enjoy their children and take care of themselves before reentering the work force.

I have more opportunities for personal growth. "I loved staying home, because it gave me so much freedom to do my own things," said a librarian who raised her three children at home during the 1960s. She went on to say that "a creatively perfect day included playing the piano, singing, writing, and drawing — as well as reading, which I always do. I made the kids have a quiet time, each by himself, so that I could, too — even after they were too old to nap."

We encourage you to look at your time at home as a parenting sabbatical. Motherhood can be seen as a sabbatical similar to the ones teachers have enjoyed over the years. The time off can be used for personal enrichment and learning. You can tackle new hobbies or skills you've always wanted to learn but never had time for before. Or you can experiment with taking a variety of adult education classes or pursue a new degree. More than 13 percent of the women in our study plan to increase their education while taking care of their children full-time, while another 14 percent will become involved in volunteer or community organizations.

Being at home can also give you more time for introspection and self-awareness, and keeping up with young children can stretch the limits of your creativity and patience. Overall, at-home mothers reported that the experience definitely changed and enriched them.

I can start my own at-home business. Being at home full-time doesn't mean that you can't bring home a paycheck. Almost 14 percent of the women we interviewed plan to develop or already have developed small businesses that they can run during their children's nap times, in the evening, and on weekends. They find it very satisfying to become entrepreneurs and to be able to continue earning an income while devoting most of their time to their children. They like the flexibility of being able to control their own work load and to work as few or as many hours a week as they choose.

These women still consider themselves at-home mothers because they have arranged their schedules and set their priorities so that they are home with their children as much as possible. Many women could not afford to stay home without the income they bring in through a home-based business. In fact, one national survey of people who work at home reported that nearly a quarter (22 percent) of all working women work out of their homes. Most of them do so so they can remain close to their children.[11]

Parenting is joyful work. Other reasons to stay home with young children are how much fun they can be and how rewarding it is to watch their accomplishments and share their hugs. "Too much emphasis has been placed on the negative side of having babies," Terry

11

Hekker says. "You hear how confining it is, that you'll be tied up and slowed down, but no one ever tells you that giving birth is embarking on a life long love affair."[12] Joyce Holte, a college professor on a one-year maternity leave, agrees. She told us, "I've never felt so adored by anyone!"

Being able to lie on the floor and play with puzzles, run around the house playing hide-and-seek, visit parks and play groups, blow bubbles, read storybooks, and play make-believe with your child can be among life's most pleasurable experiences.

Parenting is work that focuses on people, not things. Many mothers told us that since they've been home, they've had more time to nurture their friendships and family relationships. Terri Choules, a former paralegal with two young daughters, said, "When I left my job, I was actively trying to expand my circle of friends. I feel supported by the friends I've made since I've been home and am happy I've had time to develop those friendships. You don't have time for that in the work world. That makes me feel good. I know I have someone I can call when I've had a bad day."

Being able to focus more time and attention on your husband also is a benefit of staying home. One mother commented, "When I worked full-time, my husband was the last person on my list to take care of because I knew he'd understand." Now, the women we surveyed told us, they don't have to feel guilty when they get a baby-sitter and go out with their husbands because they've been with their children all day. Other women said that when they and their husbands both worked, it felt as though they were living separate lives. Since they've been home, these women have discovered a new sense of teamwork in their marriages.

Parenting is responsible work. Donna Malone said that one of her favorite parts of being at home with her children is "being able to get more involved in my community, getting to know my neighbors, and getting involved in different nonprofit organizations." Other mothers told us of their interest in environmental and political issues and their desire to make their town and society better for their children. Several women were surprised to find so many interesting volunteer opportunities out there.

Parenting is work that promotes a better quality of life. "One reason I am home," said Barbara Galli, is that "I wanted us all to have a breathing space in our lives. Every minute is not scheduled, and we have time to sit and read a book and time for a little reflection. If I were working, that would be missing. I remember the summers I had during my childhood. They were slow-paced and idyllic, and I had tons of free time. I want that for my children. I want my kids to make their own decisions about how to fill their time."

Several mothers mentioned that they want to avoid producing a "hurried child" who is pushed to excel or get involved in dozens of activities at an early age. They don't want their children to experience that kind of stress and anxiety. Mothers also enjoy not experiencing those stresses themselves. "You couldn't pay me a million dollars to leave my daughters and go back to the work-world rat race. My life is much less stressful, and I'm much more at peace with myself and the world around me," said former business manager Lois Ann Habecker Pfister.

I'm there when my child needs me. Another great advantage of at-home motherhood is the freedom to stay home and care for a sick child. A full-time mother doesn't have to call into the office and lie about the reason she needs the day off or scramble to find someone to care for her child at the last minute. In an article on the problems working parents face when a child is sick, *Parenting* magazine reported, "When the New York–based Families and Work Institute asked more than 1,700 working women to name the worst conflicts between work and family, caring for a sick child came up number one."[13]

Many mothers told us that they're grateful for being able to care for their children whenever they're needed and for knowing that their children are getting plenty of love, discipline, and individual attention. About 12 percent of our survey respondents said that they have decided to continue to stay home when their children enter school. They said that their school-age children need them as much as they did when they were babies, although they express their needs in different ways.

Victoria Harian Strella left the prestigious position of director of presidential debates for the League of Women Voters to stay home when her second child was born. She told us, "It has been a source of deep satisfaction to be an at-home mom for my oldest son in this exciting yet stress-filled year when he has started kindergarten. There's no question in my mind that he needs *me*, not a substitute care giver, when he emerges from school filled with pride or frustration and needs someone to gently debrief him on his day." Other mothers said that they plan to be home to help their children handle the turmoil of adolescence and to avoid having them be latchkey children.

By sequencing, I can enjoy my time at home and then reenter the work force when I'm ready. Every mother we spoke to mentioned how quickly the time at home passes. One woman told us, "The childhood years are so short and so precious. You only have a few years with your children before school starts, and the rest of your life is your own." Many mothers who have already established a career feel confident that they can leave the work force for a few years without causing irreparable harm to their career prospects.

Joanne Brundage, the founder and president of the national support group FEMALE (Formerly Employed Mothers at the Leading Edge), has asked, "What is this insanity of pretending you have no life outside your career? What is wrong with having kids and caring about them? With a life expectancy of 76 years, why can't women take five years out of their career to be home?"[14]

Many of the women we surveyed said that Arlene Rossen Cardozo's book *Sequencing* offers a useful pattern for mothers to follow. Her sequencing model involves three stages: working full-time, staying home with your children when they are young, and then reintegrating your career back into your life when your children are older.[15] She declares that the only way women can have it all is by doing it all, but not all at once. Sequencing women can enjoy each experience fully by concentrating on one stage at a time.

Caring for my children is my profession. Finally, most of the mothers we spoke to said that they view being a mother as a full-time job. They've decided that it's time to put their former careers on the back burner in order to get their children off to the best possible start in life. They've chosen to dedicate their lives, for a while, to being there for their family and being, as one woman put it, "a milk and cookies kind of parent."

"My children and husband ARE my career," one woman has written. "I have been blessed with a contentment I honestly believe no other job could give me."[16]

This list of reasons for staying home could have been three times as long. Space considerations limited us to presenting only the twenty benefits most commonly cited by the women we surveyed and interviewed. The implications are clear: The vast majority of mothers at home are there because they want to be and find the experience worthwhile. Full-time motherhood can be one of the most enriching and challenging careers you can choose. And while the changes in life-style and expectations are profound, so are the opportunities for joy, satisfaction, and growth.

2

Making the Decision

I have discovered over the course of ten years of
being a mom at home that it is a decision I must
choose to make every single day when I awake.
— Starla Lawrence, *part-time journalist and at-home
mother of three children*

Many women think this is the toughest decision they'll ever
make — whether to stay on the career "fast track" or to turn their
back on the workplace and head for home. Although it can seem
that way, the decision to become an at-home mother is not as black
or white as it appears. There are any number of possibilities — from
taking a few months' leave of absence to staying home for a year or
two to staying home until all your children are in school or longer —
and these decisions can be modified at any time. Often a woman
does not make a decision to stay home full-time until her second or
third child comes along.

The bookstores and talk shows are full of this year's "professional experts" telling parents what to do and what the one right
decision is. One year we are told never to pick up babies when they
cry; the next year we must run to them immediately. One year we
must keep them in physical contact with our bodies for twelve
months lest they suffer fatal "separation anxiety"; the next year we
must help them develop independence and "other-directed" rela-

16

tionships. Yesterday early weaning helped a child develop a sense of identity; today we must breast-feed until the child rejects the breast or risk raising an insecure sociopath. Yesterday all "good" mothers worked in the home full-time and were moral role models; today all "good" mothers work in glass towers and are career role models.

These fashions in child-care advice are not new. In sixteenth-century France only the aristocracy followed the custom of having wet nurses take care of their children from earliest infancy. By the eighteenth century it had become fashionable for all segments of urban society to use a wet nurse. Of the 21,000 babies born in Paris in 1780, an astounding 19,000 were sent away to be raised entirely by wet nurses until they were several years old.[1] Presumably, these 19,000 women did not think of themselves as negligent mothers. Sending children out to wet nurses was the recommended child-rearing practice of the time.

Today the media portray most parents as making the choice to send their children to day care. But that is not the only choice, nor is it the one most mothers and fathers would make if they had other options.

Of course, your decision is going to be affected by the number of options available to you in this society. While the range of options is not currently as wide as we would like (for more on the necessity of expanding your options, see Chapters 9 and 10), it is wider for this generation than for our parents or grandparents. For example, Lydia (a pseudonym), a pregnant career woman who was discussing her options with her mother, was surprised to find that although her mother and father had grown unhappy with their family life, they had never, in all their years of raising four children together, discussed their respective roles. They had simply taken a sharp breadwinner–bread baker division for granted as a given. Finally, years later, they discovered that the mother was frustrated by so much child care and the father was stressed out by the pressure to be the sole provider.

In contrast to her parents, Lydia and her husband have frank and open discussions about changing expectations, mutual fears and goals, and available options. They realize that some of the options, such as at-home father or feminist at-home mother, are

17

scary because there aren't many role models for them. This contemporary couple may be under some of the same pressures as the previous generation, but through better communication they are in a position to make better choices.

When starting to think about choices, it is important not to let the experts or society's expectations dictate what you ought to do. You must make decisions that are compatible with your own personal and family goals and circumstances. Before all else, mothers are human beings, and you'll be much happier in the long run if you take the time to evaluate your options and choose what is best for you.

First, you should know that there are a variety of approaches to deciding whether you should work outside the home or at home caring for your children. While there are some broad similarities, not every woman stays home for the same reason or comes to the decision in the same way.

More than half (51.3 percent) of the women we interviewed said that they had always known they would stay home when they had children. Contrary to the popular belief that only women in dead-end jobs willingly leave them, we found that women who establish successful careers before having children are often the most eager to stay home. They feel that they have accomplished what they set out to and are ready to take on the new challenge of becoming a mother.

One woman, whose successful secretarial career included long-term foreign assignments, said that in fifteen years in the work force, she had done everything she set out to do: traveled, earned good money, been independent. By her mid-thirties she was ready to switch careers and be a full-time mother. "Frankly," she noted, "I don't think I could have done it sooner — before I saw the world. I wonder if other women who are just starting out in a career that gets interrupted by pregnancy might worry about what they're missing by staying home. But as for me, I was ready, and I didn't resent staying home with my son for a minute."

For many women, an early decision to stay home with their children is based on memories of their own childhood. Women who grew up with happy at-home mothers are more inclined to see full-time parenting as a positive role. And some women, who were themselves latchkey children, have had firsthand experience with a life-style they do not want for their children. One woman recalls how she and her sister "hated going to the sitters, especially during the summer. We felt like outsiders all the time. Then, later, I was a latchkey kid, and as the oldest, I was responsible for the house and our safety; it was too much stress for a twelve-year-old."

Of those women who were unsure of their decision before becoming pregnant, 15.7 percent decided to stay home at some time during their pregnancy. One woman, a former editor, said that before becoming pregnant, she had only "a vague notion that I wanted to stay home. But during pregnancy, I began to realize how attached I was, literally and figuratively, to my unborn child. I knew then I wouldn't go back full-time."

Many women who initially expect to rush back to work are surprised by the depth of their attachment to — and the incredible needs of — their newborn baby. Of the women we interviewed, 11.7 percent made the decision to stay home during their maternity leave, even though they had previously made arrangements to go back to work.

One marketing manager for an architectural firm was so sure that she was going back to work that she negotiated a maternity leave and hired and trained a temporary replacement herself. "However," she said, "during my leave, when I realized just what being a new mother entails, coupled with the growing realization that this new 'part-time' version of my job would essentially be my old job boiled down to fewer hours (and no fewer responsibilities), I began to rethink my position."

This unexpected shift in priorities surprises many mothers and fathers. (We explore the changes in your relationship with your husband and the changes he will experience as he becomes more deeply involved in fatherhood in Chapter 6.)

Widespread dissatisfaction with the availability and quality of day-care services in this country is old news, and all parents experience some anxiety and frustration in their search for adequate care givers. For some parents, satisfactory services are not affordable or available. Several of the women we interviewed cited inability to find adequate day care as a primary component of their decision to become an at-home mother.

Financial stability is not necessarily the answer to this problem. Even for those who can afford live-in help or full-time nannies, trustworthy child care can be a major worry. Turnover in care givers is high, and the exact delineation of household and child-care chores is often problematic. There is also the added burden of being an employer. One well-to-do suburban mother of two told us that her family went through four care givers in one year and noted that she was getting stress headaches and her child was beginning to cry whenever *anybody* left the house.

"I will never come to peace with the lack of adequate child care I experienced as a working mother," recalled another mother. "Finding part-time, reliable, committed child care became a seemingly endless process. In two and a half years, I hired seven care givers, who quit for a number of reasons. By the end, I was paying six dollars per hour to a college student who came through an employment agency. I returned home one evening to find the entire house dark, the sitter asleep on the sofa, and my daughter lying in bed with a fever, unfed and unattended. I quit my job the very next week and swore that I would work as a cashier at midnight before I would betray the trust of my daughter's care again."

Of course, some parents manage to make good arrangements and return to the office with the best intentions, only to find that their inflexible schedules and long separations from their children still take a terrible toll on them. Attempts to comply with the traditional males-only work ethic — which requires long hours and assumes that family life is unimportant or being taken care of by someone else — can be especially frustrating. One mother recalls how both her work life and her home life suffered:

I was frustrated at work because I could no longer work those 60-hour weeks. I was frustrated at home because I was missing the opportunity to watch my baby grow. My weekends were being spent working, and I had little time to spend with my husband and even less for myself. No one at work realized I felt

I was giving up an irreplaceable experience by working, let alone *cared*. It seemed to me that while the time I spent at work meant relatively little to the company, it could mean the world to my little girl.[2]

Besides experiencing guilt and frustration, working mothers also pay a terrible price in the sheer number of hours spent on the job. Recent research indicates that working women with children put in the equivalent of an entire second shift at home — a shift that comprises most of the child-care and household chores.[3]

Of the women we interviewed, 11.7 percent tried to return to work but eventually found the situation impossible and opted for at-home motherhood. Sometimes they needed to become exhausted before they could give themselves permission to do what the old-style male work ethic wouldn't let them do: admit they were passionately involved with their children's development.

A working mother's level of frustration with scheduling and separation can rise dramatically when a second or third child comes along. Of the women we surveyed, 9.6 percent who were able to balance home and work life with one child found themselves out of balance once their family grew. One mother of two, formerly a paralegal litigation specialist, recalled, "My two-year-old, Jessica, had woken up crying in the night — again — and I found myself sobbing along with her because I thought, 'This is the only time I get to see her!' My baby, K.C., was then ten months old, and her life to that point was just a blur in my memory. That's when I decided that, no matter what, my kids and I deserved better."

Again and again, in personal interviews, through all the different stories, we heard women say, "My priorities changed. I didn't expect them to, but they did." This shift may occur at any time: during pregnancy or maternity leave and even months or years after you return to the office. It may occur even if you love your job and have, through some miracle, managed to arrange for satisfactory child care. Mary Fisk Docksai, formerly the managing editor of *Trial,* the monthly magazine of the Association of Trial Lawyers of America, told us, "It never occurred to me that I would want to be at home with my children. My plan was simply to have my baby, put him in my mother's care, and resume my career. I took five weeks off when Rick was born and hurried back to work gladly.

"It was not for some months that I began to sense the change that was occurring in me. My job became less and less important, and being with my baby became more and more desirable. One day during this time, I received the latest issue of the magazine from the printer, which is always an exciting moment. Later that day, I pulled into my driveway and honked my horn, the signal that I was home. I saw Rick run to the window and bang on it to welcome me. The joy that I felt seeing him eclipsed the satisfaction of holding a month's work in my hands.

"I quit my job shortly thereafter. I had wanted to be a mother, but what I had done was merely have a baby. I wanted more."

No matter which approach seems to fit your journey, it is the rare woman who does not experience some anxiety and conflict over so radical a change in her and her family's life. One woman described her entire pregnancy as being "filled with conflict about the future. I was so afraid of losing my identity and becoming a housewife who had no money, status, or self-worth. I left on pregnancy leave still undecided." Loath to relinquish her position and the program she managed to anyone else, she realized during her pregnancy leave that she could not relinquish her baby to anyone else, either. She decided to stay home — at least, for the time being.

The Importance of Planning Ahead

Many women who have been through the decision-making process counsel others that the biggest obstacle to making a decision is fear — primarily, fear of the unknown. While all new endeavors are usually accompanied by some fear, the key to reducing anxiety is good planning. Even the most instantaneous decision can still be backed up by good planning that can help minimize the unknown.

To plan for the possibility of one parent staying home, you and your husband must consider multiple factors, even ones that you feel uncomfortable discussing. Finances, which are usually the first question in anyone's mind, may actually be the easiest factor to get a grip on.

One Illinois couple, the Larsons, began planning to enable one parent to stay home more than a year before they even began trying to start a family. "Our goal," Victor Larson recalls, "was to get in touch with reality in order to sidestep the unavoidable slap in the face that a lack of planning might create."[4] The first thing the Larsons did was to develop a budget for living on one income. Then they initiated a trial period of one year during which their entire second income was allocated to paying off outstanding debts. Not only did this program lessen their financial burden when the transition to one income occurred, but it also gave the couple genuine insights into what lay ahead. By the time their child was born, their credit was good, monthly expenses were lower, and they already knew how to live on one income.

The trial period is the greatest boon that advance planning can give you. Not only does it teach you how to live on one income, but it also can teach you something about yourselves. Even if you are absolutely, positively sure that you don't want to care for your child full-time and will be returning to the office, you should consider a trial period because of the knowledge and insight it will give you and your husband. One way to test the waters is for you to investigate ways to earn money at home while you're still employed and see whether you can generate enough income to enable you to stay home.

Alternatively, you might try staying at home for six months or a year, then sit down and evaluate your new arrangement. At that point, you and your husband can discuss what's working, what's not working, and whether you can afford your new life emotionally and financially. If you really can't make it on one salary or if you find that you hate not having a certain amount of disposable income, you'll know before the baby comes. If you and your husband have problems to work out regarding control or ownership of income, you'll know before the baby comes.

While the trial period can be an enlightening adventure for first-time parents, for those expecting their second or third child, it can be a real hardship. Cutting back totally to one income while a large portion of the second income is dedicated to ongoing child-care expenses may be impossible. One solution is to account for every penny going to child care or other, work-related expenses such as transportation and business lunches, and then try to bank everything else.

No matter which way you decide to go, the trial period helps you come out ahead. If you decide not to stay home, your trial period nest egg can be allocated for child-care expenses or tucked away as a beginning college fund or house payment. If, on the other hand, the trial period shows you that you can make it financially and psychologically on one income, you can start your at-home parenting career with a solid base of confidence and expertise. If you don't have a lot of debt to pay off, the trial period can help you save enough income to replace a significant amount of salary and thereby buy a year or more at home with your child. This "save one year, buy two" strategy may work particularly well for parents who are expecting their second or third child, can't afford the mounting day-care bills, and want only a year or two at home until the oldest child enters school.

Advance planning also gives you time to make arrangements for a smooth transition at work. Your transition from one career to the next should be handled as professionally as possible. If you are considering working part-time in your field in the future or resuming your old career full-time after your children enter school, now is the time to make connections for consulting, part-time, or at-home assignments. If your company or other companies in your field use free-lancers or maintain lists of consultants, now is the time to put in your name. As in any job, it is better to go prospecting while you are currently employed.

It can help your credibility to meet project managers and assignment editors in a business setting while you still carry the full luster of your employment, instead of making a cold call eight or ten months down the line, with the distracting sounds of a baby crying in the background. If you are still undecided as to whether you will return to your job full-time after the baby is born, these meetings should be casual inquiries. If, however, you and your manager both know you are not coming back, you may ask your manager to make official overtures and recommendations for free-lance work.

Financial Planning

Remarkably, many of the women we interviewed reported that their family income actually went up after one parent stopped working outside the home. This usually occurred because the husband got a raise, was promoted, or actively sought a higher income by changing jobs or starting his own business, often in combination with the wife continuing to work part-time or starting her own enterprise from the house. When Loren Garofalo became pregnant with her second child, both she and her husband started planning for her transition to being an at-home mother. It took them two years to pull off their plan by paying off debts, saving money, and moving to a less expensive house in another state. When Loren started staying home, her husband entered a new business and raised their income by 70 percent.

For other families, the loss of one income means making sacrifices. It is not unusual for husbands to work an additional job, either part- or full-time. For some, living from check to check means living under the constant threat of financial ruin. One woman told us how frightening it is for her to realize that "you're only a check or two away from homelessness." This woman also has a wonderfully supportive family that helps out with occasional donations of cash, clothing for the kids, stamps, coupons, and even aluminum cans to be returned for the deposit.

These stories represent the two extremes. Most families, however, find themselves in the middle: they aren't swimming in money, but they might be able to squeak by without two full paychecks.

How do you know if you can make it? Just like any other type of financial planning, home financial planning starts with a detailed list of income and expenses, which is then used to note shortfalls and produce a budget. You probably have done this before, if not on a regular basis, at least when you figured out whether you could afford a new car or a mortgage. The important thing to remember when you are doing your proposed one-income budget is to include the costs of going to work, because after you have your child, these costs are going to increase dramatically.

For instance, one legal secretary making more than $25,000 a year was astonished to realize that after taxes and figuring in the cost of child care, work clothing, disposable diapers, and additional transportation, her cash contribution to the family income was about $8,000 a year. Now, this is not an inconsiderable amount of money, but the family quickly realized that she could bring in almost as much cash by working free-lance out of their home office. This working mother's situation is not unique. In 1991, *First for Women* magazine estimated that each year American women with children spend close to $6,000 in job-related expenses.[5]

If you want to get a quick preview of the real picture, use the simple formula in the accompanying box to estimate your real earnings after figuring in your direct work-related expenses.[6]

Calculating Your Real Earnings from Working

Salary	+	Benefits	−	Direct Expenses	=	Real Earnings
_____		_____		Taxes _____		
_____		_____		Child care _____		
_____		_____		Household help _____		
_____		_____		Transportation _____		
_____		_____		Work-related clothing _____		
_____		_____		Meals out _____		
_____		_____		Professional expenses _____		
_____		_____		Benefit contributions _____		
[ ]		[ ]		Totals		[ ] [ ]

Chart by Bruce A. Mahon

One rule of thumb is that you need to make roughly two and a half times your child-care costs for working outside the home to be economically advantageous. Of course, your detailed budget will include family expenses such as mortgages, insurance, education, taxes, transportation, savings, and vacations. You may be surprised to discover that, given the inherent costs of working, staying home with your children makes good financial sense.

For many families, life-style changes made in the name of economizing can become rewarding in themselves. "We have changed our expectations and goals," said a twenty-eight-year-old mother of three. "We have discarded the yuppie life-style of fancy homes, the latest cars, keeping up with the Joneses, et cetera, and are trying to live a simpler life. Ironically, this change in our material situation has actually made us much happier and more carefree!"

Whether by need or philosophy, many of these families expressed satisfaction in living by nonmaterialistic values and passing these values on to their children. Many husbands and wives feel that moderation and balance are some of the most valuable models they can provide for their children. "We knew it would be a struggle financially, and we have faced many hardships and problems concerning money," said Kelly Knapp, an insurance agent and underwriter who is now at home. "But I would rather be poor and be with my children than to be comfortable and be away from them. My children don't realize we're not wealthy and are very happy and content."

Besides considering "how much" you'll need to make ends meet, you also should look at "how long" your family can get by on a reduced income. Two years, until you can build up a free-lance business at home? Five years, until your only child enters kindergarten? Fifteen years, until the twins are old enough to take care of themselves after school and on vacations? Strict budgeting for only four or five years — the same amount of time you invested in your college career — may be a relatively low price to pay to get what you really want.

Values and Personal Goals

What do you really want? As you can see, while you are discussing finances, you also have to talk about values and personal goals, both material and spiritual.

Ambivalence about the woman staying home can plague families that do not bring all the issues into discussion. Wives worry that they will become household drudges, husbands crack under the pressure of being the sole support, and many couples worry about reverting to a sexist pattern of family life. As in any endeavor, these fears can be conquered only by meeting them.

The box on pages 31–32 presents some issues to think about when making your decision.

The answers to the questions listed there may not come to you right away. As subsequent chapters in this book show, you will continue to work on many of these issues throughout your time at home. But if you get these issues out in the open early, your anxiety level will be reduced, and you'll be able to make more realistic plans.

What If Staying at Home Is Not for You?

One word of warning: no matter how dissatisfied you are with alternative child care, no matter how important you feel a child's first few years are, and no matter how stable your finances look, if you do not feel that being an at-home mother will be personally rewarding for you, then don't do it. Refer to the list of the most common benefits mentioned by mothers (Chapter 1). If some of them do not ring true to you, becoming an at-home mother could be a great disservice to you, your husband, and your children.

One clinical psychologist who responded to our survey, while adamantly believing that children need to be with one primary care giver for a minimum of three months, and preferably until they are old enough to enter a regular preschool program, nonetheless feels that a decision to stay home must be voluntary. "There are women who hate being home and don't enjoy young infants, although they love their children," she explained. "If you're miserable being home and wish you were working, you're not going to give the kind of parenting you could."

If your decision is not voluntary, you will end up resenting everybody and everything. Find another way to balance your family and work life. Take as long a maternity leave as possible to find out how you'll feel as a mother at home (see Chapter 4). If you find you're dying to get out of the house and back to your desk, investigate other options. For instance, you and your husband may consider split-shift work to provide child care yourselves. Alternatively, you may ask a relative to come live with you, try to find the best day care available, or change jobs to one that provides on-site day care. Don't, however, switch careers as a sacrifice. Being an at-home mother is about *more* control of what's important in your life, not less. You will not be doing yourself or your child a favor if you resent full-time parenthood but choose to stay home out of guilt.

Full-time parenthood is not an option for women only. Sometimes it makes economic and emotional sense for the father to stay home, especially if the woman is deeply attached to her job. One couple, a nurse and an editor, decided the father would stay home with their newborn daughter and do free-lance work while the mother continued in her high-paying work at the hospital. Another couple devised an arrangement in which each took an alternate year off to provide two years of continuous care for their infant son. During his year of full-time parenthood, the father managed to finish his graduate degree, which actually led to a higher income for the family after he reentered the work force.

What do you really want? You can't ask this question often enough. One thirty-year-old programmer summed up her decision not to return to work, even though it meant delaying buying a home for several years, by saying, "I'd rather rent a room and live in somebody else's house than park my child in day care and end up with somebody else's kid."

A Final Word

One thing to remember about your decision: it's not the last one you'll ever make. The choices you make before the baby is born may be very different from the ones you will make after you and your husband are parents. The decision you make when you have only one child may be drastically different from the one you will make as a mother of two or three children. What you want today may be radically different from what you will want five years in the future, just as what you want today is probably very different from what you wanted five years ago.

Also remember that sometimes your first decision will not be the best one. Society and people change. (If you think that expectations by and about mothers haven't changed, remember that sending your child away to a wet nurse for two or three years is probably *not* one of the options you are considering.) Motherhood is a growth career. It constantly changes as the family develops. Just like anyone else, mothers have a right to change their job descriptions.

Issues to Consider When Making Your Decision

Financial Considerations

Can we make it if I quit my job? Will this ruin all our long-term plans? How much will we have to give up? Are our finances over-extended now?

Job Satisfaction

Do we both think that being an at-home parent can be satisfying? How much satisfaction do I get from my current career? How much satisfaction do I expect to get from my new one at home?

Job Attachment

How much do I enjoy the status and prestige of my job? How much of my identity is tied up in my current job?

Life-style Considerations

How will both of us react to the change? Can we both live on a budget? How attached are we to a certain life-style?

Is the Money Yours, Mine, or Ours?

Who has control of the checkbook? Will the at-home parent have an allowance? How will minor financial decisions be made? How will major financial decisions be made?

Pressures on the Working Spouse

How will you react to being the sole financial support for your family? Do you enjoy your current job? Are there opportunities for overtime or advancement? If so, do you want to take advantage of them? Given greater financial responsibilities, how will you find time to participate in family life?

31

How Can We Keep an Equal-Rights Household?

How will we achieve an equitable distribution of chores and responsibilities? Do we need to divide things up formally? Are we going to assume an automatic home/outside world division of labor? What are our responsibilities to each other and the family? Do we respect each other's roles? Are you assuming something I'm not about how this will work?

Personal and Parental Goals

What kind of family life do we want to have? Is my vision compatible with yours? What are your individual goals as a parent? A spouse? A human being? How can I help you achieve yours, and how can you help me achieve mine?

Spousal Support

Do we both share the same shifts in values? If not, how far are we willing to travel with each other on faith?

Support from Family and Friends

How much support can we count on from other family members and friends? How much flak? In the absence of support, how much more will we have to rely on each other?

What Is Best for Our Child or Children?

To the best of our ability, what kind of childhood do we want to provide for our children? Will that vision be best achieved by one parent staying home or by both parents continuing to work outside the home? Is there a middle ground? Where is there room for compromise? What is nonnegotiable? If there is already one child, what do we like about our current situation? What would we like to change? What were our own childhoods like?

3

The Four Ground Rules for Your Life as an At-Home Mother

I am evolving as an at-home mother.
I learned to make myself happy and respect myself.
— Jan Kravitz, *former sales representative and*
at-home mother

In 1984 the Center for Research on Women at Wellesley College conducted an enlightening study on women's happiness. Researchers studied three variables: employment, marital status, and children. Much to their surprise, they found that no one variable or combination of variables leads to happiness or misery. Instead, they found that the two primary components of satisfaction were mastery and pleasure, no matter what a woman's situation regarding employment, marital status, or children. The Wellesley researchers defined mastery as what makes a person feel good about herself as a valuable member of society and as a person in control of her own life. Pleasure was defined as that which makes people find enjoyment in their lives.

These findings have profound importance for anyone trying to achieve satisfaction in life. Although many of the issues mothers at home face are not unique to motherhood — after all, you can feel stressed and unappreciated in any profession — people contemplating a radical change in life-style and values often need some new ground rules. The key to success is to have a plan of action that acknowledges your humanity and your professionalism and that encourages mastery while giving opportunities for pleasure.

In this chapter we present four ground rules for life as an at-home mother. In subsequent chapters, we provide real-life examples of how you can apply these rules to help you achieve satisfaction and success in your new profession.

Ground Rule Number 1: Know What You Want Your Job to Be

What roles do you want your job as an at-home mother to encompass? Parent, teacher, cook, chief financial officer, laundress, community activist, doctor, educator, homemaker, playmate, homework supervisor, at-home entrepreneur, chauffeur, purchasing agent? As a mother at home, you're likely to take part in all these roles. In these days of increasing specialization, homemaking and child rearing may be the last bastion of the multitalented Renaissance person.

However, the multiplicity of talents the job requires does not mean that you should be locked into anyone else's expectations or stereotypes of what your job is. While it is true that all the mothers we spoke to valued their child-care role very highly and viewed it as an important responsibility, they also expressed a tremendous diversity of opinions and attitudes regarding other aspects of the job. Not all women aspire to mastery in the same areas. Most women are unwilling to buy into the 1950s "happy homemaker" image that is pervasive in our culture. Today's mother at home differs from this stereotype in having the freedom and self-awareness to make her own choices about how she wants to spend her time at home.

For example, some mothers assign considerable importance to their role as educator, even to the point of taking responsibility for total home schooling. Some — though certainly not all — women derive personal pleasure from domestic activities and are proud of being part of a tradition of domestic culture. Others focus on community activism, personal growth, or an at-home business. Whatever aspects are most important to you, the point is that you — not some outmoded societal stereotype — should decide what you want your job to be. Every job has some negative aspects, but the job of motherhood should not be so loaded with distasteful activities that you have no opportunity for pleasure. The happiest women we encountered shaped their role into one that fit comfortably with their own personality and aspirations — a finding that confirms the Wellesley research.

Ground Rule Number 2: Acknowledge Your Skills

Many women share the common fear that their skills, talents, or interests will disappear when they leave the office, that they will lose all their hard-earned mastery. However, one of the most interesting findings of the Wellesley research was that the arena in which mastery was achieved (employment, marital relations, children) was not nearly as important as the fact of mastery itself. And while new parents face an overwhelming learning curve regarding child care and their new life-style, it is important to realize that most of your mastery skills have direct transfer value. Heidi Brennan, of the national association Mothers at Home, told us that she sees motherhood as "the ultimate management challenge."

The next time someone asks you what you do all day, think about all of the professional skills you use during your typical twelve-hour workday. Mary Zastrow, a former senior computer programmer, told us, "I still view myself as a professional — a professional mother. I am constantly reading to keep up with my field, I attend conferences on mothering, and I am a member of two mothering professional (and support) groups."

Networking with other experienced mothers and keeping up with the literature are important aspects of your life as an at-home mother. Other strategies that will help you in your new profession include setting realistic objectives and goals, establishing your priorities, knowing when to delegate, working within a budget, financial planning, negotiating, organizing your household, managing your time, and training and supervising your children. Of course, you should note that children, especially infants, are not always as cooperative as colleagues, and that some of your skills and expectations must undergo considerable revision. These changes do not mean that you are without talents or resources, only that your skills are growing to meet the needs of your new environment.

A background in business can be useful for mothers at home, but business skills are not the only ones with high transfer value. Professionals from other fields told us how helpful their career skills have been in their new job as mothers. An assistant professor of speech communication said that she uses her training to analyze her child's behavior and nonverbal cues, to draw conclusions, and to listen. A graphic designer said she enjoys designing her son's room and creating toys and pictures for him.

Heidi Heinrichs told the most dramatic story of how her training as a nurse has helped her as a mother at home: "Recently, my two-and-a-half-year-old son, Joseph, climbed up into the kitchen cabinet and got a piece of hard candy. I was in the other room talking to the baby-sitter about the days I was working that week. He suddenly ran into the room, and he was completely blue." Heidi was able to save her son from choking by using the Heimlich maneuver on him.

Most of the mothers we surveyed agree that setting goals is one of the most important tools you can use to make your life more manageable — with one caveat. Many mothers find that the often recommended daily "to do" lists are actually very frustrating, since sick children or rebellious two-year-olds may prevent you from accomplishing what you hoped to. By creating a more realistic weekly or monthly list of goals, you can make some visible progress without undermining yourself.

Mothers at home also have a tremendous opportunity to extend mastery and increase opportunities for pleasure by developing new skills. This can be a perfect time to take parenting or psychology seminars, learn a sport, or consider other careers that you may eventually want to pursue. Adult education classes at local high schools or community colleges can give you plenty of intellectual stimulation while occupying only one evening a week.

Many reputable schools offer correspondence or televised courses, which can be a real boon for mothers of infants. One student-mother told us, "I was home three years and felt as though my brain was disintegrating. I finally decided to return to school (one class per quarter) and researched majors, settling on pharmacy. This has made an enormous difference in my self-esteem. It has helped tremendously to take classes and to see accomplishments that stay finished (unlike housework)."

Ground Rule Number 3: Validate Yourself

Besides fearing that they will lose skills by leaving the office, women experience a diminished sense of mastery when society does not consider the work they do in the home worthwhile. As an at-home mother, you need to find a way to meet your needs for positive feedback and self-respect.

The most important thing you can do to validate your worth as a mother at home is to find support. Unfortunately, your old office network of colleagues and friends may not be up to the task, especially if it doesn't include women in a similar situation. For this reason, it definitely helps to find other women in your situation as quickly as possible. Mothers need encouragement from one another and someone to talk with about their day-to-day frustrations, joys, and challenges.

You can find your own support network by meeting other mothers at the park, joining a play group, or joining a local or national mothers' group. Salli Gamez is an example of a woman who has made new friends and found supportive colleagues through her participation in the La Leche League. The Gamez family moved soon after having their first child, and while her husband quickly met new people through work, Salli met no one for more than a year. "Now," she said, "I know more people than my husband does thanks to La Leche League. I also serve as a La Leche leader. My phone is so busy I can't handle all the calls and had to get an answering machine."

Another strategy for self-validation is to find a mentor. You don't necessarily have to join a group if you're not the joining type. Sometimes even one other mother you can talk to can make all the difference in easing your transition to being at home. An experienced mother who has been at home for a while can be particularly helpful, since she can serve as a sounding board and role model. A friend you can call at any time and ask, "Why won't this baby stop crying?" or "What do I do when she hits her brother?" is worth her weight in gold.

You also can validate yourself by seeking out circumstances and situations that reaffirm your values, goals, skills, and work. The bibliography at the end of this book is a good place to start a literature search, and community organizations such as the Parent-Teacher Association (PTA) and school board are usually respectful of people who take child development seriously. Basically, you take your validation where you can find it. We know many women who won't miss an episode of "Roseanne," the perfect nineties antidote to all those years of "Ozzie and Harriet."

Finally, the most important component of the validation you need in this new phase of your life is your spouse. If he shares your values and appreciates your contribution to the family and its quality of life, you will have your most important source of validation.

Ground Rule Number 4: Consider Yourself a Feminist

Historically, the feminist movement has been accused of not respecting mothers at home. As columnist Anna Quindlen notes, "There has always been a feeling on the part of moms that the Women's Movement has not taken them seriously, has in fact denigrated what they do, unless they do it in a Third World country or do it while running a Fortune 500 company and the New York marathon."[1]

A significant portion of the women we surveyed said that they feel personally let down by the women's movement and that the message feminists gave them while they were growing up was that staying home to raise children is a waste of a woman's life and education. There is historical precedent for this perception.

During the 1960s, in the early days of the movement, the emphasis was on opening up options to women outside of the home. The mythology of the time deemed that the proper place for a woman to use her talents was as a housewife and mother; other avenues were not open to her. It was not until a decade later that Betty Friedan criticized her earlier book, *The Feminine Mystique,* for being oblivious to issues of family and children.

During the 1970s, the focus moved to opening up opportunities outside of the home in the business world. In the 1980s, the public emphasis was on advancement and equal pay for equal work.

In the late 1970s and early 1980s, however, even as the politically active arm of the movement focused on workplace-related issues, serious feminist thinkers began to reexamine mothering and family life. While media attention focused on demonstrations and workplace issues, a rich body of feminist literature on mothering was steadily growing. The list includes poet Adrienne Rich's *Of Woman Born,* Nancy Chodorow's *The Reproduction of Mothering,* Dorothy Dinnerstein's *The Mermaid & the Minotaur,* Jane Lazarre's *The Mother Knot,* and Betty Friedan's *The Second Stage.* In 1979 the National Organization for Women (NOW) held the historic Assembly on the Future of the Family. Unfortunately, this aspect of the feminist movement did not get as much media attention as the headline-grabbing political aspects.

In the late 1980s, the emphasis began to change once again to a critique of societal pressures that limit women's choices, such as the workaholic male-oriented corporate culture. Whereas the focus was once on getting women into the traditional man's world, today it is beginning to change to altering that world to accommodate men and women and empowering both to make choices. Increasingly, feminist thinkers and activists are deeply concerned with quality of life and parenting issues. Instead of changing women into men, the focus is on changing a patriarchal society to make it more amenable to women's needs and contributions.

If we are to situate organized feminism's current attitude toward motherhood, we would have to define it as clearly pro-women, pro-options for women, and pro-credit for women's work, whatever it may be. The key concept is freedom of choice. The movement will support a woman in her work, whatever that may be, if the woman has chosen it freely. The great feminist issue of the 1990s will be the acknowledgment of the value of a woman's work, wherever and whenever she does it — in the office, factory, studio, field, farm, or home.

Can you be a full-time mother and a feminist, too? The answer is "Yes, absolutely," even though some women still experience the separation that occurred when the feminist movement seemed to leave behind women who took motherhood seriously. This division is damaging to the movement because the basic philosophy of feminism affirms and supports all women's search for mastery, success, and self-fulfillment.

One mother in our survey commented, "I really feel the feminist movement is about supporting women's choices. For me to take time out and be with my kids does fulfill the ideals of feminism. It's OK to have time for work and at-home motherhood at different times in your life. You don't have to take sides." If a woman chooses to use her talents in the domestic arena for herself and her family, instead of in the office arena for someone else, feminism should affirm that choice.

One of the lessons feminism has taught women is that their needs are important and that they must make time for self-development in addition to caring for their families. Feminism affirms the right of women as human beings to pleasure and personal growth — one of the Wellesley study's components of satisfaction.

Finding time for yourself can be a problem when your workplace and your relaxation place are one and the same. This is a problem mothers share with other people who work at home. When you sit down to read a book or strip down for a soak in the tub, or whatever it is you do to relax, you are surrounded by undone tasks and the pitter-patter of small emergencies on eager feet. Feminism tells us that like any other worker, you are entitled to time off. Whether your alternate care giver is your spouse, a relative, a paid baby-sitter, or a colleague from the baby-sitting co-op, you are entitled to your leisure time without guilt or interruption.

Considering yourself a feminist does not mean that the only achievements you can make are in the work force. Raising children at home and doing the job to the best of your abilities may be the most valuable contribution you can make. As Suzanne Chambers, a former advertising and sales promotion manager, put it, "I'm trying to raise my daughter as a feminist, something I wouldn't trust an outsider to do. I hope she will realize that my choice to be a professional mother is part of my feminist philosophy. I chose this job because I felt it was the most important job I could do in my life."

Now that we've gone over the ground rules, let's see how they apply in your everyday life. In the following chapters, we look at some of the internal conflicts and external pressures that trouble mothers at home. Then we explore how these four ground rules can enable you to combat your own, and society's, negative expectations and misconceptions.

4

Making the Transition

Making the decision [to stay home] was easy, but
the transition was very difficult.
— Maryann Wegloski Cooke, *former accountant and
at-home mother of two young sons*

So You're Home — Now What?

No career is without its challenges, large or small, and motherhood is no exception. The transition period in any new job is likely to be fraught with some anxieties as you adjust to the demands of a new pace and schedule. As a full-time mother, your performance will be measured in far different terms at home than at the office, and the very idea of what you're accomplishing on the job can be in for a radical change.

Everyone tells you that as a new mother, you'll be sleep deprived, moody, overwhelmed, exhilarated, and depressed, in turn. As a professional woman turned at-home mother, though, you'll face more adjustments than just learning how to care for a new baby. If you've been in the work force for several years, you may face a difficult transition in giving up your title, salary, and business accomplishments in favor of family life. Like Maryann Wegloski Cooke, you may feel delighted with your decision to stay home, but the first several months after leaving your job still may be hard as you work at creating a new life for yourself as an at-home mother. In this chapter, we discuss some of the conflicts and difficulties you're likely to encounter and offer ways to apply our ground rules (see Chapter 3) to help you make a successful transition to your new life.

Whether you decide to stay home right after the birth of your first child or when your children are older, motherhood requires trade-offs that are more significant than simple schedule adjustments. New mothers face a lack of sleep, uncertainty about how to care for a baby, and the "baby blues." Professional women, at whatever point they opt to stay home, also struggle over whether they've made the right choice, frustration with their loss of freedom, and mourning for their old selves and buried careers.

"The transition from professional work to home life was surprisingly difficult," said Ursula Smith, one of the mothers who participated in our survey. "It was total culture shock, and I was in foreign territory." We heard the phrase *culture shock* again and again when mothers explained how they felt about being home for the first few months.

For most women, being home is about as different from their previous careers as you can imagine. In many ways, it's like going from a large, bureaucratic corporation to working for a freewheeling, entrepreneurial partnership. All the rules and structures you're used to at work have changed, and it takes time to get adjusted. Ironically, although at-home mothers have more control over their relationship with their child, they often find that their new career includes chaotic, disorganized schedules, irregular work hours (with plenty of overtime), no clear job assignments, no performance evaluations, mundane chores, few coworkers, and obviously, no salary. For women who have been used to being in control of their time and of themselves, this can be extremely frustrating.

Susan Wynn, formerly a legal secretary, described the transition from working woman to at-home mother this way: "Suddenly a once productive individual is reduced to a state of total disorder by an adorable bundle of joy weighing in at less than ten pounds but requiring ten times the attention of the toughest two-hundred-pound boss. Your work hours, which you thought were long before, have now stretched to twenty-four a day (with a few hours' sleep grabbed whenever you can), and the five-day workweek has become seven. There's no feedback, no compliments, no paycheck, and none of the satisfaction that comes from completing anything!"

What makes this transition even harder is that most mothers feel as though they're the only ones having trouble adjusting. This is particularly true for at-home mothers. In our research for this book, we came across dozens of books written for employed mothers, but very few that address the concerns of mothers who choose to stay home.

Life at home also can be a shock because so many professional women never thought they'd end up there. They put all of their effort into advancing in a career and never even considered staying at home until a baby came along and changed their priorities. Families have been getting smaller, and couples now routinely delay having children until their thirties, so many women today have little direct personal knowledge of what it's like to raise children. Some haven't held a newborn since their baby-sitting days or ever. For that reason, they may feel very unsure when it comes to running a house and raising a child. It can take a year or two of on-the-job training before you feel confident that you are doing a good job as a mother.

Great Expectations

Expecting is not limited to pregnancy. Both first-time mothers and experienced mothers who have recently left the work force expect the most unreasonable things of themselves as at-home mothers. They assume that taking care of a baby will not be very difficult and will leave them with lots of free time to explore their own projects. They imagine that the house will be sparkling, they'll have cookies in the oven, and they'll still have time to read to their children and work on their dissertations. In addition, women who have chosen to stay home when their second or third child comes along often have the unrealistic idea that they'll make up for everything they missed with their older children. Unfortunately, things aren't that simple.

Children are notoriously indifferent to their parents' hopes for a structured life. They stay up all night teething, get double-ear infections at the drop of a hat, won't nap when you're begging them to, fall asleep when you're longing to get out of the house, and get a strong dose of stranger anxiety the very week all your relatives descend for a visit. Loraine Goodenough, a mother of two who has her own word processing business at home, thinks it's all a plot to keep you on your toes: "As soon as you figure out what schedule the baby has you on, the baby is *honor-bound* to change the schedule."[1]

In addition, much of the most important work that is done with children, especially newborns, has absolutely nothing to do with schedules or productivity. You may spend an entire morning lying on the bed with the baby squeezing toes and saying "Oooo, oooo" back and forth. This is exactly the type of essential response-stimulation activity that develops attachment, empathy, language, and a sense of competence, but it is not going to further that work on your thesis, if your intention was to whip one out during this period.

Beth Lindsmith writes about her frustrations as a new mother in *Parenting* magazine: " 'I'm not getting anything done,' I would wail, wild-eyed, when my husband came home at night. . . . I blamed myself: I still must not be organized enough. If I were more disciplined, I reasoned, I could plant shrubs, finish *Anna Karenina*, learn Italian, and still have ample time for motor skills development exercises with the baby."[2] These unrealistic expectations are especially common among women who are used to running a department, managing a sales force, or doing other challenging professional work. You used to be able to accomplish all your goals. Why, you wonder, is one little baby making it almost impossible to do *anything?*

One mother we surveyed said, "I didn't realize how little free time I'd have when I had my first baby. You wonder, 'What's wrong with me, that this is taking so much time?' You almost feel embarrassed to ask other mothers. You ask them about teething, but not the important questions." Most women don't realize how much time and energy it takes to be a full-time parent until they become one.

Struggling with their own expectations is not limited to new mothers. Women who decide to stay home full-time several months or years after their first child is born may find it harder than they expected to come to terms with the change in life-style. Mothers of two or more children also go through a transitional period each time they welcome a new baby home. One woman told us, "I had just got into a routine with my oldest when the second child came along (they're just sixteen months apart). I'm just starting to feel comfortable now, and they're four and a half and three. It was really tough for the first two years, but now we feel like a family."

Don't lose heart. It is possible to make time for yourself. (We talk more about that later in this chapter.) But remember to be flexible in setting goals for yourself. Many at-home mothers who were professionals in the workplace and were used to working sixty to seventy hours per week underestimate the amount of time a newborn demands and overextend themselves trying to do all the projects they've been putting off for years. They burn out just at the time they need the most energy.

Any business manager should remember that one of the best ways to keep employees' morale high is to set realistic, achievable goals. Heidi L. Brennan said that she and the other leaders of Mothers at Home have found that "whatever you think will take you two weeks to do without kids will take you six weeks as a mother. As long as you have realistic expectations, you won't disappoint yourself."

Other false expectations can cause havoc for new at-home mothers. Women who expect life with their child to be perfectly blissful are doomed to disappointment. There may be days when you wonder, "What am I doing here? This is no fun at all." If you can make it past the first six months or so, you generally see a big improvement as your child begins to be more responsive and active. But you'll face new challenges when your child becomes a toddler, a two-year-old, and so on.

Other women expect that their lives can continue as they were and that having a child won't change things too much. One mother commented, "I remember thinking that when I'm home on my maternity leave, I can meet all my friends for lunch and go to the pool every day. I expected I could have my own life, just as I did before, and would just have an extra person along. I was surprised when I didn't experience that." As we mentioned before, a baby's or young child's needs and desires often collide with your own. You don't have the freedom to come and go as you please, which you used to take for granted. And it can be difficult to suddenly be totally responsible for another person's life, health, and happiness.

If you can adjust your expectations and accept that you'll have good days and bad days as a mother (just as you had your ups and downs at work), you'll stand a much better chance of making a smooth adjustment to home life.

New At-Home Mothers of Older Children

Much of the discussion to this point has dealt with women who leave the work force as soon as their first baby comes along. Mothers of older children who are staying home for the first time face some different challenges in becoming accustomed to their new role.

More and more women are reconsidering their decision to work away from home when their children are older. One mother of a four-year-old and an eight-year-old who recently decided to stay home noted, "It was easier to be away during the day when my children were babies. Now they have their own ideas and feelings and are emerging as interesting individuals. I don't want to miss this chance to spend more time with them."

Those mothers who have been working outside the home for a matter of months or years may find it very hard to relinquish their ties to the working world. They have established professional achievements, friendships with colleagues, and independent lives as career women. Leaving all that behind to stay home, however much they long to be with their children, is not easy. Most women particularly miss having private time. A marketing executive said, "I miss going into the office, having a cup of coffee, and being my own person for eight to ten hours."

Juggling the needs of two or more children is a challenge that many mothers are not prepared for. Often women make the decision to stay home after their second or third child is born and day care gets more expensive and complicated. Even so, staying home is not always the ideal solution. The timing can be less than auspicious. Women may find themselves coping with toilet training a stubborn three-year-old while trying to calm an infant with colic. Children who were used to spending time with their parents only in the evenings and on weekends may become more clingy and demanding once their mother becomes available during the day.

Kirsten McKay spent long hours working in retail management until her son turned four. For a long time she had been thinking about staying home and suddenly decided that she was ready to leave her job. To swing it financially, she needed to earn an income as a day-care provider. She faced a doubly difficult transition in getting used to caring for several other children, getting them on a schedule, and finding ways to spend more personal time with her son.

Kirsten told us, "The woman who cared for my son during the day told me she was going to go back to teaching school in the fall. And I thought, 'Oh, no, who'll take K.C. to preschool? And how can I throw him into another day-care situation?' Then I thought that maybe I could do it. I realized that as he grew older and got involved in more things, I would miss every T-ball game he played in because of my work schedule, and I would miss so many other parts of his life. The breaking point came when he had chicken pox and my boss said, 'I'm sorry, you'll have to come in.' I was torn. I knew I should be there for him. The women I've worked for who don't have children just don't understand a parent's priorities.

"So I thought I'd try staying home, and I'm so glad I did. I found several children who needed day care quickly, mostly through word of mouth. I probably work longer hours now than I did before — the first child arrives at seven A.M. and the last one is picked up at six. But it's different. I answer to myself and don't feel the sense of competition and pressure I had in the work force.

"It has been an adjustment and hard for K.C. because all the other children are around and sharing my attention. If I'm talking to him and a baby cries, I have to go pick her up. But it's better than my not being there at all. You do give up a part of yourself when you give up a career. It's ingrained in you — you're constantly striving to get ahead. But I decided to channel my energies into the day-care business, and that's made it easier."

Leaving work to stay home is not always a tough transition. Sometimes it can be surprisingly smooth. Annie Mahon worked as a consultant and saleswoman for a large software company after the birth of her first daughter. When she learned she was expecting twins, she thought a lot harder about staying home. She told us, "I felt no guilt about leaving my job because the doctor said I had to — I needed to go on bed rest for the last few months of my pregnancy. Although it was hard to be alone and not be able to go out and do anything, it was easier than I expected it to be.

"When the twins arrived, I was so busy being responsible for three young children that I really didn't miss my work. Although I liked being busy and active in my career and got to travel a lot, it all seemed to pale in comparison as soon as I stayed home. It didn't seem bad when I was working, but as soon as I stopped, I realized what I had missed. I didn't know everything my daughter was doing during the day, how many things she learned each day, and how much fun she could be.

"Right now I'm working from home two days a week, and that's working out very well. I have a lot less responsibility in my job now, and that's fine with me. I just want to do what I have to do in the hours I have to do it in and then get back to what I really want to do: be with my kids."

The Biggest Challenges At-Home Mothers Face

When we asked, "What is the hardest thing about being a mother at home?" we found that women who enjoyed careers outside the home before staying home with their children struggle with some nearly universal problems. We don't want to trivialize these problems by suggesting that there's a simple, one-sentence solution for each one. However, the women in our survey provided some excellent coping strategies for getting through the transition. Keep in mind that everyone's situation is different. Apply your own creativity in solving these problems — then write and let us know if you have found any helpful strategies you'd like other mothers to know about.

Putting Your Career on Hold

This can be a wrenching experience, particularly for women who are ambitious and have achieved a certain level of success after many years of hard work. If you've recently left the work force, you will probably miss the camaraderie with coworkers and the challenges you used to face in your job. It also can be a big adjustment to go from being a respected career woman to being viewed as "just a mother at home." Laurie Koblesky, former editor in chief of *Video Times Magazine,* said, "It didn't hit me until my baby needed less constant attention and I had time to think. Then it dawned on me how much I'd given up. I missed my friends at work first, and then I missed the work. I didn't realize how much I was tied into my achievements until I stayed home."

Formerly employed mothers can really miss such joys as regular paychecks, lunch and coffee breaks, their professional status, bonuses and promotions, business travel, and adult conversation. Once they're home, many mothers also worry about reentering the work force and wonder how they will explain a five-year (or longer) gap on their résumés.

Loss of Direction and Structure

Women in the work force are used to having their days structured for them. Once you're home, you're in charge of structuring your own life and setting goals for yourself. If you don't, your children will do it for you. When you're getting used to being home, you may get up in the morning and think, "I don't have anywhere I have to be today," and that can be scary. One mother said, "I was sitting in my rocking chair soon after I came home, watching my one-year-old son playing on the floor, and I thought, 'What do I do now?' There are almost too many options, and mothers who are used to the controlled environment of the workplace can feel paralyzed when trying to decide how to spend their days.

Boredom and Household Drudgery

Household chores are a sore point for most of the women we talked to. It's hard to find them satisfying, and they get undone very quickly. In addition, you can spend so much time doing housework that you don't have time for the things you really want to do. It's never ending. If it's not the laundry, the kitchen floor needs to be scrubbed. In spite of all your efforts, one or two children can make the house look like a disaster area in a matter of minutes, without even trying.

If you're not careful to make time for your own interests, being home with a young child can be boring. Dealing with dirty diapers and picking up toys all day can be pretty tedious. As an executive secretary now at home put it, "It's much easier to go to work and deal with people who speak English and have control of their bodily functions." Women who are used to challenging work can get very frustrated with repeating everything over and over again each day, and they can feel as though they're stuck in a rut.

Dealing with Constant Interruptions

Being home with preschoolers can mean never being able to finish a thought or a conversation, let alone reading a book from cover to cover. Many mothers surveyed said that due to the recurring nature of housework, they struggle with feeling that they haven't accomplished anything in their time at home: "You start a job and never finish it"; "The worst part is not being able to get things done and feel satisfied"; "There's no sense of progress; you start all over at square one every day." For women who are used to seeing projects make steady progress (even if they have to cope with countless department meetings), being interrupted all the time can be maddening.

Ground rule number 1: Know what you want your job to be (see Chapter 3) can help when you're facing the four problems listed here. Remember, you're starting a new career as a full-time mother, not taking an extended vacation from your former occupation. Missing the status and perks of your previous job seems less galling when

51

you consider that your new career at home has its own rewards — especially the ability to spend limitless quality time with your children and the freedom to make your own decisions about what you want to accomplish without anyone looking over your shoulder.

This freedom from outside structure can be frightening at first to women who are not used to it. But the feeling of drifting through your life at home without a sense of direction usually passes quickly as you find a new network of women with children, join play groups and baby-sitting co-ops, or take YMCA or community group classes with your children. After a while, as you get more and more involved with activities in your community, you may long for those unscheduled days.

Household chores aren't much fun, but keep in mind that you don't have to spend all your time on your hands and knees if housework makes you miserable. Decide what you want your job to be and then devote most of your time and energy to more fulfilling pursuits for yourself and your children. Housework is a necessary evil that can and should be shared with your husband and family. Contrary to outdated images of at-home mothers, modern mothers do not make cleaning the focus of their lives.

As for living with constant interruptions, if you chose to stay home because you wanted to nurture your children and participate in their education and development, dealing with constant questions and demands is part of your new job description. Although it can be frustrating, your availability to your children makes an enormous difference to their sense of security and self-esteem.

Feeling Inadequate as a Mother

Most new mothers sometimes feel at a loss when learning how to care for their child. Mothers of older children who decide to stay home also may feel inadequate when faced with their children's all-day demands. This is especially true for professional women who felt competent and had confidence in their skills at work but feel helpless when confronted with a crying baby. "As someone who was always well trained to do my job (and successful at it), parenting has been a very humbling experience," said Missy Attridge, an attorney. "I find it more of a challenge than practicing law and am often frustrated by how little training there is for this relentlessly demanding job."

As in any new job, the uncertainty can be overwhelming at first when you don't know what you're doing. One mother remembered that "the worst part was feeling I wasn't good at this job. I wondered, 'How do I play with this child? What do I feed her?' I just didn't know how to go about mothering." Having the desire to be a perfect mother also can lead to feelings of failure. You may find yourself setting unrealistic standards for yourself or second-guessing how you handle things with your children.

Loss of Identity and Self-Esteem

New at-home mothers are often haunted by the question, "Can you be a viable person without a title and a paycheck?" Women who have defined themselves by their occupations and enjoyed the prestige of their corporate positions may feel as though a part of their identity has died.

Trying to retain a positive self-image can be especially difficult because of the stereotypes many people have of mothers at home. Falling into the stereotype of centering your life on your husband and children can make you wonder whether you're neglecting yourself. Self-doubt also can make you question your sexual identity. One mother admitted, "I felt a lot of insecurity at first. I never thought I'd worry about my husband and those other women in the work force. Now that I'm home, I wonder, 'Am I still attractive?' "

Other women worry that they'll lose their professional identity permanently. Donna Malone works one day a week as a marketing research executive. She said, "After leaving full-time work, I was afraid I'd lose the skills I'd built up in business and lose my confidence in myself."

Staying Intellectually Active

Many women fear that once they stay home, their abilities grow rusty and their mind will turn to mush. Susan McDonald writes, "Nothing is more terrifying to me than the progressive loss of my intellect! It seems like another person who once got a degree magna cum laude in a scientific field. Now I forget what I drove to

53

the store to buy! I'm beginning to feel like I'm sacrificing myself for my children."[3] Several of the women we surveyed said that one of the things they miss most about their former careers is the intellectual stimulation they enjoyed on the job.

Ground rule number 2: Acknowledge your skills (see Chapter 3) offers some answers to these three problems. As we pointed out earlier in this chapter, everyone feels some self-doubt and uncertainty when they begin a new career. This is true whether you're switching from journalism to teaching or you're changing from business manager to at-home mother. As in previous job changes, you will quickly gain expertise and confidence by performing your new job. Finding mentors or colleagues who can answer your questions and allay your fears can be a great help when you're feeling inadequate as a mother.

Although you need to take some time to come to terms with your new identity as an at-home mother, remember that your character, skills, and experience don't disappear with your last paycheck. You can transfer the skills and positive self-image you earned at work to mothering, community work, and other activities. Once you are at home, by looking beyond a narrow self-definition based on what you do, you have the opportunity to gain a deeper sense of self and identity based on who you are. This crucial issue of identity and self-esteem is explored in much greater detail in Chapter 5.

Staying intellectually active may not be easy, but watching your brain turn to mush is not inevitable. You might find that your at-home years are a great opportunity to explore new ideas and interests. You don't have to let your hard-earned professional skills and educational accomplishments fade away. Finding ways to exercise your mind through book groups, adult education classes, mothers' groups, community work, and continuing involvement in your occupation or professional association will make it easier to revise your résumé and reenter the work force when you're ready.

If you don't plan to return to paid work for many years, you can participate in a variety of activities you enjoy without worrying about how they'll look on a résumé. Learning new skills while you are at home can give you a sense of satisfaction and accomplishment — just as it did while you were in school and the office.

Isolation

Almost every mother we surveyed said that feeling isolated is her biggest problem. After losing their colleagues at work, women often feel friendless as they get used to their new job at home. Unless you make a big effort to get out and meet people, you can face days on end with no one to talk to but young, uncommunicative children. (When we asked, "On a typical weekday, how many adults do you have face-to-face contact with other than your spouse?" over 15 percent of our respondents answered "none" and 20 percent answered "one.") This is particularly true for mothers who live in rural areas or in a neighborhood where most of the women work outside the home.

In some cases, isolation can make mothers feel so psychologically depleted that they find it hard to cope with anything. One mother said that "getting used to being at home was horrible. I had no friends. I was real depressed and lonely. I tried going to the park, but I was always the only mother on my own; everyone else was in pairs. I felt there was something wrong with me." It wasn't until this woman joined an at-home mothers' support group and heard other women make the same observations that she began to be able to cope with her situation.

Feeling Trapped

Many women said that when they worked outside the home, they were out of the house for twelve or more hours a day. They never got to know their neighbors and weren't used to being confined inside the same four walls. These problems were compounded for women who had newborns in the winter months and felt completely housebound. Patricia Velkoff, a family therapist, told us, "When I worked full-time, I was literally never at home. I'd leave at six A.M. and return at eleven at night. I liked being active and involved in a lot of things, and the idea of being at home all day was frightening to me."

Loss of Old Friends and Coworkers

It's common knowledge that once you become a parent, you have less in common with old friends and may find it hard to maintain your friendships. One problem is that you're both doing different things now and don't have convenient times to get together and talk. By stepping out of the business world, you also leave the life you used to share with coworkers. One mother told us that leaving work "took me out of a lot of conversations. It almost made me feel like I wasn't as important as everyone else." Other women said that they feel as though their old friends find it boring to talk about their children and don't share their new priorities as parents.

Lack of Rewards and Recognition

Most mothers don't get much positive feedback. In fact, they're often showered with negative reactions, from crying babies to unwanted advice from mothers-in-law. It can be very difficult to find satisfaction in such a thankless job after being used to recognition in the workplace.

As a mother, you no longer have regular performance evaluations, raises, or promotions, which helped you gauge your abilities and accomplishments. A teacher told us, "One of the difficult things about being an at-home mother is there's no immediate positive feedback. I was always a good student. When I went back to school for some continuing education after my daughter was two, it was so ego gratifying to get a good grade again. I felt I produced something that was recognized as a good product. Parenting is not like that."

Feeling Powerless

Many women who used to wield power and influence in their former occupations feel as though they don't count anymore. Jan Kravitz, previously a sales representative, said, "I've been feeling a lack of 'important' decision-making power these days. All I seem to decide about now is little things. When I worked outside the home, I made decisions concerning my clients, career directions, itineraries, strategies, etc. Now my decisions are: How often do I really need to vacuum? Will hubby like this casserole? Should I start brushing Beth's teeth?"[4] This feeling is compounded by people who view at-home mothers as nonworking women who are not worthy of their attention.

Lack of Respect from Family, Friends, and Society

Life at home can be hard for some of the reasons we've outlined. But feeling looked down on by others can make it even harder. Many mothers feel that when they're introduced to someone new, unless they mention their former occupations, they'll be seen as lazy women who can't get a "real job." Women in the work force, in particular, tend to have skewed ideas of what a mother does all day at home. Elise Sillers said, "I just got off the phone with a working (nonmother) friend of mine who always asks if she was interrupting my nap! There are many misconceptions about us."

Other women said that they're infuriated when they're not taken seriously. "When I do get out and away from the children, I usually don't want to talk about the brand of diapers they use," Stephanie Michelle Ansberry, a marketing assistant who decided to stay at home with her children, told us. "I have more scope than that, and I get frustrated that people don't recognize that fact. My extended family is quick to dismiss my opinions and analysis of events because 'all I do' is stay home. I no longer qualify as having informed opinions. This can be very stressful for me." The mothers we surveyed still feel that society does not value the work they do at home, and they often find themselves having to justify their choice.

Ground rule number 3: Validate yourself (see Chapter 3) can make these conflicts easier to handle. When you're feeling isolated from your old friends and coworkers, build up your confidence by finding, joining, or creating networks of like-minded women with children. It's very difficult to be happy at home if you don't have friends who can lend a sympathetic ear and understand how you're feeling. See Chapter 8 for an up-to-date listing of both national and regional mothers' support groups.

Also, becoming an at-home mother does not mean that you're a prisoner inside your home all day. There is a wealth of activities out there, but it does take some initiative to participate in them. Most communities have a YMCA, park, or library that offers "mom and tot" story hours and classes in gymnastics, swimming, dance, music, free play, art, and so on. If you're not sure your child is ready for such organized programs, try planning your own field trips to nearby places of interest.

Since positive feedback can be hard to come by in your new job, it's up to you to give yourself your own pats on the back. Setting challenging goals for yourself and sitting down every now and then to evaluate your progress can help you find a sense of achievement. You might even want to put your objectives in writing and give yourself an annual performance review, just as you used to experience in the workplace.

Unfortunately, many people have stereotyped views of at-home mothers as dim-witted housewives who do nothing but watch talk shows and soap operas all day. Don't let the outside world convince you that you're no longer a contributing member of society just because your home has become your workplace. If you respect yourself and think of yourself as a professional mother instead of "just an at-home mother," others will be more likely to take you seriously. We discuss the issue of fighting societal misconceptions in Chapter 5.

Role Conflicts

The mothers in our survey cited conflict over traditional sex roles as a big problem. After spending years considering themselves independent, modern women, they fought against falling into a housewife role after giving up their paid work. Husbands and wives who have established patterns of sharing chores and household responsibilities may find themselves at odds over renegotiating their duties. Wives often resent husbands who expect them to do all the household chores because they're home all day and "don't have anything else to do." We discuss this further in Chapter 6.

When you become an at-home mother, other people, even friends who know you well, may assume that you've turned into a traditional wife whose husband makes all the family decisions. Creating a workable marital and family pattern without falling back on old stereotypes can be a challenge.

58

Loss of Financial Independence and Not Having Enough Money

"I miss having a paycheck with my name on it *so much,*" one mother said with a sigh. Being without your own income can upset the balance of power in your marriage and make you feel as though you no longer have an equal voice in the family. Mothers can feel vulnerable about being dependent on their husbands and guilty whenever they spend money on themselves. A Chicago area mother said, "I don't like feeling dependent at all. It's hard to come to terms with. I'm frightened that my husband might lose his job, now that there's only one paycheck. And I feel like it's not my money to pamper myself with anymore. I know intellectually it's my money, too, but emotionally it's very difficult to accept."

Most families with at-home mothers are troubled by financial constraints just as their expenses are skyrocketing. They must deal with the stress of wondering whether they will have enough money to pay their bills each month and of having to find new ways to conserve the family finances and live on a tight budget.

Feeling Guilty About Your Choice

It's easy to feel guilty about so many things: "wasting" your education and your potential, not contributing financially to your household, putting a burden on your husband. One woman said, "I've realized that I'll feel guilty no matter what I do. I thought that if I didn't go back to work, I'd be guilty of not making extra money to spend on the baby. But if I did go back to work, I'd feel guilty about not being with the baby. And now, if I don't get everything done in a day, I feel guilty."[5]

Some mothers we surveyed said that they feel as though they are letting down the women's movement: by giving up their paid employment, they are not encouraging younger women to be independent and have their own careers. A mother of two preschool girls commented, "I got upset when my daughter said, 'Daddy's working. Mommy doesn't work.' She doesn't understand that this *is* my work. I'm upset when I read articles saying that working mothers are the best role models for girls. And I think, am I failing my daughters?"

59

No Time for Yourself

Time off is one of the most beautiful phrases in the English language to an at-home mother, probably because it's very hard to come by. Mothers with infants literally work around the clock for months. When their children are older, full-time mothers remain on call twenty-four hours a day. (Forty-two percent of our survey respondents said that they work fourteen or more hours a day caring for their children. Sixteen percent said that they get no help with child care in a typical workweek.) Even for women used to working long hours in an office, the amount of energy needed to be a mother can be a shock. Heidi L. Brennan remembers, "I was overwhelmed by all the physical demands of pregnancy, delivery, and baby care. I kept thinking, 'Will I ever have my life back? Will I ever have a free hand again?' "

If you've been employed and were used to long, empty weekends and regular vacations, doing without them can be the hardest part of your job as a mother. When you have one child, you may have some time to yourself during nap time, but it's hard to accomplish anything when your child can wake up and demand your presence at any moment. When you have two or more children, you may never have any time during the day when all the children are napping or otherwise occupied. Michele Miller, a bookkeeper at home with a six-year-old, a three-year-old, and a newborn, told us, "My husband was complaining about having to work a twelve-hour shift the other day, and I said, 'What do you think I'm doing every day?' And *he* gets twenty-some dollars an hour for those twelve hours!"

Most mothers can't even take a sick day when they need one. Some mourn the passing of pleasures such as going shopping by themselves, having a quiet meal in a restaurant, being able to sleep late in the morning, and coming and going as they please.

No Time for Your Husband

Husbands can feel neglected when children come along. Although you may spend a lot of time together as a family, you and your husband may have very little time alone — except when the children are asleep and you're worn out too. Women also feel pulled in two or more directions when both their children and their husbands are clamoring for their undivided time and attention.

Some couples struggle to maintain their intimacy after the addition of a child has upset the status quo. Sexual desire and opportunities for sex can be in short supply, particularly with infants and toddlers around. Unless husbands and wives are careful to communicate, they may find themselves growing apart because they no longer share a focus on their careers in the work world. "Conversation with my husband is more difficult now because I have a limited range of daily experiences to share," Sylvia Reese said. "How often does he want to hear about nap times and feeding schedules?"

Ground rule number 4: Consider yourself a feminist (see Chapter 3) comes into play with these dilemmas. Being without a salary for a while does not automatically make you the second banana in your own family. It's important to discuss these issues openly with your husband and remind him of your contributions to the family. To avoid being treated as a dependent, insist on an equal say in financial decision making as well as equal access to the household checkbook.

By the same token, don't assume that you are now the chief cook and bottle washer — as well as chief diaper changer, clothes washer, grocery shopper, housecleaner, and so on. When you both worked for pay, you probably shared household chores, and there's no reason to discontinue that arrangement now that you are at home. In fact, caring for young children can be more time-consuming than most outside careers, so you need your husband's participation at home more than ever. By taking the time to examine each of your assumptions about your roles within the family, you may avoid ending up with an old-fashioned domestic division of labor. It's better to come up with a solution that takes into account both of your skills, interests, and available time for household work.

If you're struggling with guilt over whether you've made the right choice, remember that all that anguish isn't getting you anywhere. All guilt can do is wear you down and make you question your own self-worth. Choosing to raise your child yourself is nothing to be ashamed of — quite the contrary. Enlightened feminists agree that there's much more to life than advancing in the workplace. By showing girls and young women that a woman can make her own life choices at home and at work, you can give them a solid foundation for making their own decisions when they reach adulthood. That's being a positive role model!

You don't have to settle for not having any time for yourself and your husband. With the freedom to structure your own time comes the responsibility to make sure you're allowing yourself enough time off for personal growth and enjoyment. Make sure you plan some time for yourself every week, either through shared baby-sitting with a friend, hiring a sitter once a week, participating in a "mom's day out" program in your community, or signing up your children for preschool classes as soon as they reach the age of three. You can't expect to be a good mother by sacrificing yourself. It's important to make some time every week to meet your own needs as well as those of your family.

Finally, keep in mind that this, too, will pass. On bad days, when your children are sick, whining, or fighting with each other, remember that being home with young children is not a permanent condition. Your job will grow and change as your children grow, and they do that very quickly. This thought also helps you savor the good times with your children. They won't be around long to snuggle in your lap, nor will they always consider you their favorite playmate. And you probably will return to paid employment, with all its stresses and challenges, once your children are older. Enjoy your time as a full-time mother while it lasts!

Conclusion

In this chapter, we've explored all the tumultuous feelings you may experience during the transition from the workplace to the home. Remember that these feelings of self-doubt and anxiety don't happen only to mothers — they accompany all major life changes and may recur when you or your husband retires or when your children leave home. By applying the four ground rules explained in Chapter 3, you can maintain your sense of self in the midst of this turbulent transition and find some solutions to the frustrations you face as an at-home mother.

Changing Relationships: Starting Over with Your Husband, Family, Friends — and Yourself

5

Creating a New Self-Image

Helmer: Before all else you are a wife and mother.
Nora: That I no longer believe. I believe that
          before all else I am a human being.
                         — Henrik Ibsen, *A Doll's House*

Stereotypes versus Reality: The Motherhood Myths

The new at-home mom is not only out of the office and into
the nursery; she is also out of her old self-image and into a new one.
For a professional woman whose self-image may be intimately tied
to her job description, this change can be devastating. Besides the
usual stress that comes with any new job, she knows that our
culture does not put much value on the job of homemaker or
child-care provider and actually promotes negative images of these
vocations. This negative climate can make the at-home mother's task
of creating a new self-image, which should be a joyous work of
personal transformation, more stressful than it need be.

Messages about what others think of us — either personally or
as members of society — can help or hinder our self-image. Of
course, the final touchstone is always yourself, but it would be naive
to assert that you can ignore cultural and interpersonal messages.
Professional women and businesswomen, who are used to a lot of

feedback from their colleagues, supervisors, and society about how well they are doing their job and who define themselves by their job titles, may be particularly affected by the larger culture's perception of their new career.

In this chapter, we discuss at-home mothers' experiences with stereotypes versus reality, give practical advice on how to deal with common myths about motherhood, and show how creating a new self-image can be a positive growth experience.

In this country, a job is not just a useful source of income. Most Americans derive their identity and self-worth from the title on their office door and the salary they command. Because at-home motherhood is an unpaid position, these mothers are often referred to as nonworking. This description, as we have seen, is untrue.

The cliché of the idle, lazy housewife sitting at home watching soaps is pervasive, as is the image of the household drudge wielding her mop and broom and worn down by an endless cycle of cleaning, cooking, and changing dirty diapers. At-home mothers, as portrayed in television commercials, are stuck in the 1950s mold of small-minded housewives. They may not wear aprons and pearls anymore, but they are usually presented as women who are more concerned with lavishing attention on their houses than on caring for their children. Interactions with children are usually characterized by guilt and worry, not competence and satisfaction. These women are easily worked up to a fever pitch of anxiety by a yellow shirt collar or a spotted wineglass, and they glow with fulfillment when the house is sparkling clean.

Modern at-home mothers who have left successful, established careers to nurture their children find it very hard to see anything of themselves in this picture. The stereotype of the hysterical, childish adult female obsessed with cleaning is blatantly false, yet the makers of these commercials persist in presenting it (though they are much more sensitive about not producing commercials that portray other negative cultural or ethnic stereotypes).

In contrast to this negative image, there simultaneously exists the idealized Victorian image of the perfect full-time mother: always nurturing, compassionate, even tempered, and wise, selflessly sacrificing herself for her children and her husband. Contemporary culture has added gourmet macrobiotic cook, home-based business executive, and crack tennis player to this impossible portrait.

Women who choose full-time mothering today are likely to spend a great deal of their emotional energy walking a cultural tightrope between these two equally ridiculous and unachievable stereotypes.

What are at-home mothers *really* like? Results from our survey reveal that they are neither idle and pampered nor perfect Betty Crockers of the home front. They do work hard — 42.2 percent said that they care for children fourteen hours or more per day — and their twenty-four-hour on-call factor is higher than that of any other profession (except, perhaps, medical interns). Almost one-fifth said that they don't get time off during the workweek. Things are only a little better on the weekend, as more than 36 percent of the respondents reported that they don't get any time off then, either. In fact, full-time mothers have very little free time in terms of what workers have come to think of as their rightful time off   a period during which you have no responsibilities to a boss, employees, or coworkers, you are on your own, and you can do what you like.

The image of the idle, decorative country club wife also is very far from the truth. According to our survey, only 3 percent of at-home mothers have more time for sports or exercise. And while the economic profile of these families is solidly middle class, they definitely are not the idle rich: half of them are supporting three, four, or five people on less than $40,000 a year and are constantly searching for ways to economize. A small but dedicated minority — about 8 percent — is making do on $20,000 a year or less. And as for those long, lazy afternoon naps, forget it! Only 1.7 percent said that they or their husbands get more sleep. More than 14 percent of the women we surveyed said that they get less sleep than in their prechildren days.

Most mothers at home are neither youngsters, inexperienced, nor unskilled. They are not at home because they have failed to make a go of it in the business world and have no other career options. Half of them have undergraduate degrees, and nearly 40 percent have advanced graduate, professional, or technical education. More than two-thirds of them fall into the thirty- to forty-year-old age bracket. As a group, they were very productive and

69

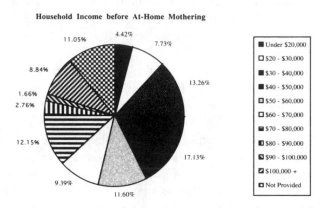

Household Income before At-Home Mothering

well-paid workers. Most had household income in the $30,000 to $40,000 range before leaving their previous jobs.

Having children did not turn these women into immature, incompetent, lazy emotional wrecks. The decision to stay home with their children was not made at the mercy of hormonal assaults on their IQs or during the depths of some postpartum depression. For 51 percent of them, the decision was based on a rational, value-based evaluation made before they even got pregnant. These women are staying home because, as they noted in our survey, they "believe it is the best way to raise a child," or because they "don't want to miss their children's childhood," or because they want to "raise their children themselves with their own values," or simply because they have such a "strong emotional attachment" to their children that they couldn't leave them. Under 3 percent reported that they are staying home due to a lack of adequate alternative child care.

What's more, as a group, these women are overwhelmingly positive about the choices they have made. More than 97 percent said that they have no regrets and that if they had it to do all over again, they would make the same decision.

Household Income after At-Home Mothering

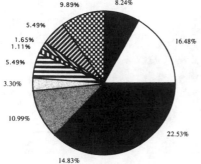

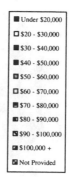

- ■ Under $20,000
- ❑ $20 - $30,000
- ■ $30 - $40,000
- ■ $40 - $50,000
- ■ $50 - $60,000
- ❑ $60 - $70,000
- ◪ $70 - $80,000
- ▥ $80 - $90,000
- ◪ $90 - $100,000
- ▨ $100,000 +
- ◪ Not Provided

The portrait we have drawn of an informed, experienced, talented, well-educated, hardworking at-home mother is certainly a positive one. Why, then, when we asked at-home mothers how they feel about themselves, did the picture change? Why did almost a third of them report conflict in their own self-image? In interviews, why did they come back again and again to their fears of becoming a drudge, less of a person, a dependent, a nonadult?

Part of the answer may lie in the women's response to our question, "What was the hardest part about leaving your former job?" About 24 percent said the predictable thing: "Loss of income." About 22 percent said it "wasn't hard at all." But surprisingly, more than 28 percent said that "loss of identity and professional status" was the hardest part.

We suspect that at-home mothers experience conflict and doubts about their self-image because, despite the reality of their situation, the impossible cultural stereotypes and concurrent loss of status persist. At-home mothers continue to walk the tightrope.

Walking the tightrope can be especially precarious for new mothers, who need all the emotional energy they can get to deal

71

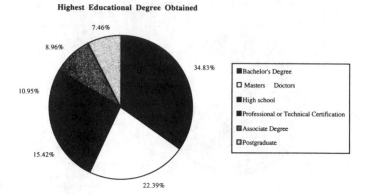

Highest Educational Degree Obtained

7.46%

8.96%

34.83%

10.95%

15.42%

22.39%

- ■ Bachelor's Degree
- □ Masters   Doctors
- ■ High school
- ■ Professional or Technical Certification
- ▨ Associate Degree
- □ Postgraduate

Charts by Bruce A. Mahon

with the demands of intensive child care. Psychologist Jane Swigart, who writes extensively on the emotional experience from the mother's point of view, points out:

> The continuous offering of physical care, protection, and empathy can cause care-givers to feel not simply fatigue but acute emotional deprivation. In this country, many mothers feel such extreme impoverishment they become vulnerable to disturbing forces both within and without: depression, rage, guilt (for who can feel anger toward a defenseless beloved infant who needs you?) and feelings of worthlessness which come from our culture's devaluation of the intensive labor of child-rearing.[1]

Dealing with Motherhood Myths

How can a mother at home successfully negotiate the stereotype tightrope? The first step is to realize that your self-image and sense of self-esteem will be assaulted by assumptions that the culture — and maybe even you and your family — make. We call the inability to see through these stereotypes *mother blindness,* similar to color blindness. Mother blindness occurs when we let preconceived ideas cloud our vision of the real woman we encounter and see her only as a generic mother. Our selective blindness means that we are unable to see her for what she really is.

For example, one woman told us, "People give lip service to mothers and apple pie. But when I'm walking down the street with three little kids, I get a lot of reactions. Either they think I'm a saint (which is absurd) or I'm an ignorant person who doesn't know how to use birth control. I've been asked, 'What are you, a baby machine?' "

Of course, recognizing mother blindness is not enough — you also need strategies for dealing with it in a way that can educate the "blind" person while simultaneously supporting and enhancing your own developing self-image as an at-home mother. Here is where the four ground rules come in again. Let's see how they can help you in some typical situations.

Motherhood Myth Number 1

Your husband or friend assumes that you don't really work and asks, "What do you do all day?"

Most of the work that mothers do at home is invisible — not because it doesn't happen, but because the culture refuses to acknowledge it as work that requires skills and talents. A typical list of the skills, activities, and responsibilities of an at-home mom might run as follows: chef, chauffeur, medic, purchasing agent, nanny, nutritionist, teacher, supervisor, financial manager, psychologist, interior decorator, gardener, seamstress, and social director.

No matter how much expertise and labor this list represents, a fact of life in this country is that the work performed by women in their own homes is not counted as work. Consider this: even if a woman performs in the marketplace services that carry a high dollar value — designer, chef, purchasing agent, doctor, counselor — the minute she leaves the office and performs the same services at home, the dollars disappear and the work has no status. It becomes invisible. The government doesn't tax it, the gross national product doesn't measure it, and most employers don't accept it as evidence of experience or expertise. Of course, if this work is invisible, it doesn't exist, and people are going to ask, "What do you do all day?"

Work done in the home and the acknowledgment of the skills required to do it was not always invisible. In fact, the traditional nuclear family of the 1950s (man as the sole breadwinner, woman taking care of the home and children) and the harassed, dual-career parents of the 1980s (both parents working outside the home, children and home cared for by a succession of paid care givers) are both fairly new family models.

Prior to the Industrial Revolution, when masses of people left their homes and farms to go work in factories, work and skills used in the home were acknowledged as important because the home was the focus of economic activity. Cooking, canning, weaving, spinning, education and rearing of children, stores management, and animal husbandry were all recognized as being essential to the economic vitality of the family unit.

Even *upper class* did not necessarily mean *leisure class*. The diaries of plantation mistresses and castle chatelaines record an endless stream of household management tasks, in some cases equivalent to being the general manager of a small city.

With the advent of the Industrial Revolution and increased urbanization, the center of economic activity moved from the home and farm to a separate workplace. Work in the home, which women continued to do, became invisible.

Of course, there is no going back to the Dark Ages. And few people, men or women, would give up the conveniences and accomplishments of our modern world. But we must realize that work in the home still goes on, though its nature has changed.

Instead of being a place where goods are created, the home today is more about arranging for goods and services — in short, home management, something businesswomen should find quite familiar. And the basics of child rearing — which requires love, attention, discipline, education, and nurturing — haven't changed at all. If motherhood and homemaking are to stop being the invisible profession, mothers have to fight the assumption of invisibility by actively acknowledging their skills.

One word of warning: Remember that the question, "What do you do all day?" *can* be asked innocently — a request for a narrative of how your day went. Or it can betray ignorance and an unexamined acceptance of the motherhood myth of the lazy housewife. How can you answer this question constructively? Assuming the question is not innocent, one option is to take an aggressive approach. You can turn the sentence around and ask, "What do *you* do all day?"

Alternatively, you can have a routine answer that emphasizes your key responsibilities: "I take care of my child and manage my household." If the situation warrants detailing, give specifics of tasks: bathe, feed, and play with my child; do marketing, budgets/books, and household chores; have meetings with my child's teacher; organize a baby-sitting co-op; take my child to the doctor; comfort my child when she is sick; plant a garden; and so on. Some women put their own style of humor into this detailing approach; one woman told us that she says, " 'I had a long conversation over whether dragons and magic are real and went down the slide fifty times today. My children and I go to the zoo, preschool, and the grocery store, make messes, and hang out together.' "

Another approach is to ask, "At what time?" While people usually do only a few things in an office, one of the hallmarks of child care is the wide-ranging, multitasking nature of the caretaking. For example, at seven in the morning you're a cook; at nine you're playing games; at ten you're a doctor; at eleven you're doing household tasks; at noon you're a cook again, or maybe a laundress; at two, if the baby naps, you might be a writer, a business consultant, a seamstress, or a reader; at three you're discussing child care with your colleagues at a play group; at four you're doing marketing; at five you're simultaneously trying to cook and play blocks; at six you're eating; at seven it's bath time; at eight you're reading stories. All day long, no matter what else you're doing, you're giving your child comfort, care, and guidance. By giving an answer this detailed, you might be able to get the message across that parenting is a complex, challenging job.

Whatever the strategy of your response, the important thing to remember is to be positive and apply *Ground rule number 2: Acknowledge your skills.* If you don't do that, your work will remain invisible to others and to yourself. Never describe, to others or to yourself, what you do this way: "Nothing — just play with the kid and run a few errands."

One mother struggling with stereotypes admitted that it is very hard for her to explain what she does "in a way that seems meaningful." She tries to "laugh it off. If I try to explain to them the minute details of what I do, it doesn't sound like much. 'I cook a few meals, pick up lots of scraps of paper, say no twenty dozen times and say good job thirty dozen times, and maybe have a few minutes for myself.' "

This woman's summary of her day doesn't seem to project much confidence in her work. Contrast her reply with another woman's: "I look them straight in the eye and answer proudly, 'I'm at home with my children,' and then I mention my leadership in a mothers' support group or my writing."

Unfortunately, even women who present their work in a positive manner may still run into incomprehension. One woman told us, "I read them a list of everything I'm involved in. I tell them, 'I'm on the board of this and that organization,' and I mention everything I do outside the home — although my most important job is staying home and raising my kids. But that doesn't seem to be enough for other people."

It is a fact of life that you will always run into people like that — no matter what your work is. If the acquaintance is casual, forget it. If you are applying the ground rules, the encounter shouldn't affect your self-esteem. If, however, this is a relationship you want to keep, you can apply *Ground rule number 3: Validate yourself* by taking the preemptive approach and making sure others understand the scope of what you do by having them do it. One mother told us that she often invites friends who don't understand her life at home to spend some time with her and see what it's like. She thinks it's much easier to show them her daily activities than to try to explain them all. While you wouldn't want to leave your child with a casual acquaintance or business associate, you will be amazed at the new appreciation for your job that close friends and family will develop if they take care of a couple of toddlers for a day.

Of course, some women are lucky enough not to run into demeaning stereotypes, as in the case of the mother who told us, "Fortunately, when you have twins, people don't usually ask you those insulting questions. I say, 'I have twins at home,' and they shut up."

Motherhood Myth Number 2
A woman who leaves her job is told she is "ruining it" for other women because employers won't be willing to hire women if they "only leave to have babies."

In this situation, you really need to apply *Ground rule number 4: Consider yourself a feminist* and point out that there is a double standard at work here. Recent studies indicate that women actually miss fewer days of work and change or leave jobs less frequently than do men. Statistically, women are still a better employment risk than men.

The reasons men and women change jobs may be different, though. Although both sexes may leave or change jobs due to promotion, job switching, or family relocation, men have a higher incidence of leaving a job due to alcoholism or disability, while women have a higher incidence of leaving a job to have children. The net loss to a business is the same whether a worker leaves to take care of children or enter a drug treatment program, but no one accuses the alcoholic man of "ruining things" for all men. Men are seen as individuals, while women are still viewed as a subclass held to different standards based on stereotypical attitudes instead of facts.

This double standard is especially ridiculous when you realize that in Europe, where for years long parental leaves and even shortened work weeks for parents have been the rule, and where many more men take advantage of the right to time off to care for children, women's "employability" has not suffered in the least.

By the turn of the century, women will represent more than

half of the American work force. Maybe by then a several-year parental leave will be an option for all parents. In the meantime, don't let anyone criticize you for following a career path that isn't based on the male corporate workaholic model or hold you to standards that are unfair or unequally applied. Fight them with facts.

Motherhood Myth Number 3
The work mothers and homemakers do doesn't have worth.

As long as the work done in the home is invisible, it will be hard for at-home mothers to feel a sense of accomplishment, especially if they are used to receiving a paycheck every week that tells them exactly what they are worth in the marketplace. How can mothers feel a sense of accomplishment and combat assumptions that what they do doesn't have worth? They can apply *Ground rule number 3: Validate yourself.*

At-home mothers who see themselves as the family servant or "just a housewife" are doing themselves and their new profession a terrible disservice. Columnist Anna Quindlen explains:

> I wanted to be somebody, and now I am — several somebodies, to be exact. And one of them is Mom, who has job responsibility for teaching two human beings much of what they will know about feeling safe and secure, about living comfortably with other people, and with themselves. . . .
>
> I love my work. Always have. But I have another job now and it's just as good. I don't need anyone to validate me anymore, with a byline or a bonus, which is a good thing, because this job still doesn't get much validation.[2]

If Quindlen, a talented woman who is lucky enough to make her work visible through a nationally syndicated column, is still concerned about validation, consider what a profound problem this is for the rest of us!

Of course, it is possible to add up the theoretical salaries of the various job descriptions that at-home mothers fill and assign a dollar value to them. Full-time working parents who have to pay for others to do this work are well aware of the expenses involved. For instance, in metropolitan areas the cost for child care alone often runs more than $200 a week. Even "Dear Abby" has tried to put a price on the value of a homemaker, which she estimates at approximately $52,000 a year.

But the whole point for at-home mothers is that, if family finances permit, they want to employ their skills at home for their own families, and not in the open marketplace. What then are they worth?

If we are still talking about a dollar value, recent divorce settlements based on the concept of *equitable distribution* are a good indicator. In the book *What Is a Wife Worth?* lawyer Michael Minton describes the premise behind equitable distribution. The family is an economic unit, a partnership. A wife can acquire property rights (house, business, and so on) as a result of her contributions as a homemaker.

An Illinois judge's 1981 equitable distribution ruling states: "To succeed [a marriage] depends on an alliance of husband and wife. Often the marital estate is the result of this mutual effort. The fact that one party's contribution to the estate can be readily quantified in dollars in no way maximizes that party's interest over the other's."[3] In this case the woman, whose contribution could not be readily quantified in dollars, was awarded half the family farm.

So it is possible to value in dollars what an at-home mom's contribution is worth. But most of us would like to stop short of divorce as a way of becoming visible and finding out what we have accomplished at home.

What is harder — but much more important — is valuing what an at-home mom is worth in terms of quality of life. Especially during the 1980s, our cultural assumption was that worth and quality of life were measured in terms of material possessions. There are signs that that assumption is beginning to change, from professionals who are downshifting their careers, to the increasing number of at-home mothers, to surveys of young people who say a happy life is more important than getting ahead.

How much would it cost you to replace an irreplaceable relationship — the one between you and your child? What price can you put on being there when your child says her first word or takes her first step — not to mention all the other milestones and moments of everyday life? What is it worth to you to know that if your child is sick or hurt, he has the best attention and care? What is the reduction in stress, anxiety, and worry that results from no longer having to juggle child and office worth to you and your family?

None of these benefits has a price set in the marketplace, and only you know their worth to you and your family. Don't fall into the trap of assuming that because the marketplace doesn't put a value on something, it has no value. Apply *Ground rule number 3: Validate yourself.* Make sure that, in the absence of a paycheck from somebody else, you have opportunities to celebrate and confirm your worth.

Perhaps, like one woman we know, you could keep a private journal to record precious moments, experiences, and achievements. Other women get a great deal of satisfaction from setting goals for themselves and their families and then checking tasks off the list when they accomplish them.

Opportunities for validation also can come from your family. Many families we know have regular family meetings to organize chores and schedules. If you already have or are considering instituting family meetings, make sure that you talk about and celebrate quality of life issues at this time, not just problems.

Public opportunities for validation are available through play groups and mothers' groups. In these associations you will find colleagues who will appreciate and value your work.

Motherhood Myth Number 4
People think that what you do isn't work and ask you, "Don't you miss working?"

Wanda Marie Block, an at-home mother with a two-year-old, gets very frustrated when asked by friends when she is going "back to work." She says, "Do people think my life's been on hold for the last two years? This *is* my job — this is my life. The last two years were a difficult adjustment from career world to motherhood. My 'career world' memories are just now fading. But I enjoy being my own boss, spending the day with my daughter, visiting with other moms, and running my household. I am the heart of my family. I now know that I am doing one of the most important jobs in the world: shaping a child's life — my child's life!"[4]

Block is successfully applying the first ground rule: she knows what she wants her job to be, even though others may not agree with her. She could go even further and validate herself by saying to her friends, "Why, I'm working now! I miss thus and so about my previous job and love thus and so about my current job. I feel my work is going well. How are things going with your job?"

Motherhood Myth Number 5
Others assume that a woman loses all her ambition, goals, and competitive drive when she stays home.

Acknowledging the skills you use on the job as a mother does not mean denying other skills that may not have anything to do with mothering. You need to acknowledge the other skills that are still part of your personality and self-image. Make sure that you don't relinquish your competitive skills and needs when you become a mother, and find an arena to display them. Every woman needs a chance to feel that she is challenging herself and accomplishing something.

A mother of three young children in our survey acknowledges her competitive drive and teamwork skills by playing on a women's softball team. She told us, "This is the best team I've ever played on. It's very gratifying to be with people who play well, to feel part of the team effort, and to play well yourself." Another woman decided she wanted to try competing in a triathlon and trained hard for most of one year. She took part in two triathlons and performed very well. These activities enabled her to acknowledge the drive for success that she had honed in the workplace.

Competition does not have to be physical. Another woman found the courage to submit several poems to a poetry contest, even though she had been shy about showing them to family or friends. When she won the contest, she not only received a prize but also added to her self-confidence.

Motherhood Myth Number 6
A woman's opinion isn't valued because of the work she does. Perhaps someone she meets at a social gathering drops her when she says that she is an at-home mother.

The vast majority of the at-home mothers we interviewed reported some degree of nervousness and conflict when introducing themselves to new people. How do you describe what you do? How can you honor your current job but also acknowledge the full scope of your interests and skills? *Ground rule number 3: Validate yourself* can help. Tell people that your current job is full-time mother, homemaker, or whatever term you prefer. Never preface that term with "just a"; that is how you *invalidate* yourself. If you would like to add, "My previous job was . . ." or "I also serve on the school board," feel free to do so. There is no betrayal of motherhood in letting people know the full scope of your interests.

Some women never run into this particular problem. Cathy Marie Wolcott told us, "I have never had someone put me down for being an at-home mom. Perhaps this is because I always speak positively about what I do. I use enthusiasm to stop negative comments before they come. I find people then go away with the impression that I like what I do and that being at home is important to me."

Motherhood Myth Number 7
Since a mother is at home full-time, the house, the children, and the woman herself are always expected to be perfect.

Unfortunately, this myth may be self-imposed, as women buy into the stereotype of mother-as-ring-around-the-collar-avenger. As Martha L. Petersen, a secretary who is now an at-home mother of two preschool boys, put it, "I never feel as though I'm good enough, and I feel so much pressure to be perfect. I feel as though my self-image is entirely wrapped up in my home and my children. If my home isn't spotless or my children are ill-mannered, it reflects poorly on me." Part of knowing what you want your job to be is setting your own performance levels and ignoring the image that the motherhood mythology and television commercials promote.

Some women also report guilt about wanting time off or time

What Do You Call Yourself?

We were surprised at how many different answers there are to this question. Here are some of the responses from our survey.

- "I usually say 'full-time mother' instead of 'at-home mother' because I'm never home but a lot of my life revolves around being a mom."
- "I say, 'Right now, I'm at home full-time with my kids.' I preface it with 'right now' because this isn't a terminal condition."
- "I say 'domestic engineer.' At-home mother doesn't cover enough. If I have a few minutes, I say, 'I'm a nurse, a cook, a social secretary, family accountant, et cetera.' "
- "For a long time, I said an editor because that's my former profession. I like the term *at-home mother,* but it doesn't encompass all that I am. I feel it's limiting. I want to say, 'I'm that, but I'm also this.' It's because of the stereotypes attached to it. I tend to rebut them before anyone says anything."
- "I say, 'I stay home with my children.' I don't have an identity problem with the terminology of staying home. I don't need to say, 'I'm a working mom — but I work at home.' But I am also happy to say that I do free-lance work and that I'm not exclusively a mother."
- "I say, 'I used to work in an office, and now I'm fortunate enough to stay home with my daughters.' When I say it positively, I find that people don't bug me about it."
- "I say, 'I care for my children at home' or 'I work at home.' I taught my son to say that he and I work at home, and Daddy works at the office."

for themselves. After all, they're supposed to be mothering full-time, and that must mean twenty-six hours a day, eight days a week. At-home mothers need to give themselves permission to have a bad day and to be tired, bored, or frustrated, just as in any endeavor. One thirty-seven-year-old office manager, who has been home for six years with her four children, has finally settled into a balanced attitude about her job's performance levels: "Some days I do it very well, and some days not well at all." The important thing is, she's doing it, and on her terms.

Motherhood Myth Number 8
Others assume that you live a lazy life of leisure, spending all day in front of the television.

In *A Mother's Work,* author Deborah Fallows recalls how outraged she was the day a telephone solicitor called and tried to sell her a subscription to *Working Mother* magazine. When Fallows told him that she was now at home with her children, the solicitor tried to sell her *TV Guide* instead![5] Some women report that former coworkers view them as being on an extended vacation. Again, making sure that you acknowledge your skills and show pride in your work when you talk to others can help to prevent these misconceptions, though it's impossible to avoid them entirely.

Motherhood Myth Number 9
Taking care of children makes you juvenile and limits your interests specifically to child care.

One of the mothers we interviewed commented, "When people find out you're a mother, they think you can only talk about potty training. Although I consider myself a well-read person, in some circles when I'm introduced to people as a mother of three, they see me as a blob. Having a job indicates you're an intelligent person. If you don't have a job, you have to prove it."

Having to prove it, not only to casual acquaintances but even to close friends and family, is something that many at-home mothers experience. The irony is that at-home mothers often are better informed than the average person. Not only do they read a wide range of magazines and books regarding their biggest project — child rearing — but they also are often well-informed about local politics, education, and medical issues.

One woman, who regularly listens to in-depth news analyses and interviews on her local National Public Radio affiliate, usually finds herself more knowledgeable about national affairs and economic trends than the full-time businesspeople she meets at parties or PTA meetings. "These fast-track commuters don't even have time to pick up the daily paper," she explained, "while I consider it part of my job to stay informed so that I can do long-range planning for our investments and future projects. They may try to dismiss my opinions initially, but very few of them make that mistake twice. After several years of doing this, it doesn't bother me too much if a new person doesn't take me seriously. There are plenty of others who do, including my husband, my children, and myself."

An accountant who recalled how devastated and miserable she was when she first quit the work force, said that it helped her immensely "to know that other women with a college degree quit to stay home." This satisfied at-home mother is applying *Ground rule number 3: Validate yourself* by seeking out mothers' groups where she can meet other parenting colleagues who can confirm her self-esteem as an intelligent woman.

Often all you need to get through an uncomfortable situation is a firm grasp of *Ground rule number 1: Know what you want your job to be.* Lori Stillwagon, a mother of three who's been home for five years, told us, "I'm not always perfectly happy. I get little respect from my husband's coworkers. I know people who think they're talking over my head and explain things to me! But in my heart, I know what I am doing for my children is my best. *They matter.* The work colleagues, the strangers — they don't really count. When I realized that, I became more at ease and less defensive about mothering."

Motherhood Myth Number 10
People dismiss all mothers who stay at home as traditional, conservative women who don't believe in women's equality.

A *Fortune* magazine cover story titled "Can Your Career Hurt Your Kids?" paints an alarming picture of how parental overwork and inadequate day-care centers may be harming the next generation. The article does not, however, present staying at home as a realistic solution. Instead, it suggests that this option of "rolling back the clock to an idyllic past" is proposed only by a growing band of conservative social thinkers who are simply "out of touch with the economic temper of the times."[6]

The reality is that many at-home mothers are liberals or feminists who believe in raising their own children, not necessarily conservatives who believe that a woman's place is in the kitchen. Heidi Brennan, codirector of Mothers at Home, said, "At-home mothers are an incredibly diverse group. And it's very frustrating and hard to communicate that to the media. My pet peeve is all the references to 'Ozzie and Harriet.' You're seen as either a modern or traditional person, as either working or at home. But I'm both; I work at home. And my life may look traditional, but I am not a subservient housewife. Most mothers I know have partnership relationships. It's not the king of the castle and the maidservant."

The truth is that all mothers interested in having their work valued and honored can be viewed as feminists, whether their political orientation is conservative, liberal, or radical.

Self-Esteem and Self-Concept Dislocation

The myths we've explored in this chapter make many women feel as though they've been cast adrift when they become at-home mothers and cause them to wonder whether they still have identities of their own. We are not talking about the profound shift in identity and responsibility that occurs when anyone, no matter what their situation is, becomes a parent, but the subtler, more insidious issues of self-esteem, autonomy, mastery, and self-image that accompany the transition to full-time parent. At support group meetings it is not unusual to hear new at-home mothers make statements such as this: "I used to be a chemist, and now I'm a mess."

The story of Audrey is one example of what can happen to a woman's self-esteem when she becomes a full-time parent at home. An elementary school teacher, Audrey confessed that "I feel a lot of conflict and guilt as an at-home mother." Audrey's husband and many of their friends are professionals, and when Audrey is with this group, she feels "terribly useless and a failure. Emotionally, I feel like I did not achieve all that I, as a woman, should have."

Audrey is not the only person to struggle with "Who am I now?" questions. Terri Cavi, a merchandise manager at home with a three-year-old son, said, "I truly believe I'm doing the best thing for my family, but sometimes I wonder what I'm doing for myself. I worry that my whole life now is centered around my husband and son, and I'm frustrated that I'm kind of losing myself. All of me is spent giving to somebody else. Right now, I'm searching for who I really am, other than a mother or a wife."

Terri and Audrey, and many other at-home mothers, are ex-periencing what psychologists term *self-concept dislocation*. Self-concept dislocation occurs when a major event in a person's life forces her to radically change the way she looks at and thinks about herself.[7] In the book *Sequencing,* Arlene Rossen Cardozo makes the point that when a woman's "entire being is tied up with her occu-pation and then she leaves her job, she cannot help but suffer feelings of loss, anxiety, and even grief. These are the same feelings experienced by the man who, at retirement, finds himself bereft because he has *been* his occupation and now feels that without his job he's without a self."[8]

Like the retired man (for whom society has a lot of sympathy), the dislocated woman must now look at herself as a person, rather than as her occupation. For some women, this experience can lead to a profound identity crisis that is both terrifying and liberating. Sherri McCarthy, a reference librarian now at home with her chil-dren, said that she really "had to grapple with the issue: What *was* I now that I was no longer a librarian and did not have a paying job? What made my existence worthwhile? I had to find some intrinsic worth in myself simply as a human being — which is something I had not given a great deal of thought to since the probing, exploring days of high school and college."

The good news is that if your self-esteem has generally been high, the low self-esteem brought on by a self-concept dislocation will probably be short-term.[9] If you have a history of success and self-confidence to build on and use the ground rules in Chapter 3 to keep your vision of your new work unclouded by stereotypes and mythology, all you will need to do is revise some aspects of your self-image to reflect your new life.

The first step in this revision is to get a good grip on the profound psychological differences between work inside and outside of the home. As we have stated before, work outside of the home usually revolves around firm schedules, money, and productivity. It also is public, with many formal support structures and relationships; relies on group processes and decision making; is concerned with control of processes, products, or services; and has relatively short-term quantitative goals. In contrast, work at home with children is repetitive, solitary, and informal; has few support structures; is involved with nurturance and influence rather than control; is intimate and emotional; and has long-term, qualitative goals.

If you are trying to maintain good self-esteem based on a self-image that depends on the first set of characteristics while you are engaging in an endeavor and life-style characterized by the second set of characteristics, you are headed for trouble. You will most likely have a severe case of self-concept dislocation. No matter how high your self-esteem was before, you will have a hard time recovering from this dislocation because the standards you set for yourself are not compatible with your new life.

Reestablishing Your Identity

For most of us, however, the adaptations do come. Linda Rush, codirector of FEMALE and a marketing manager at home with a four-year-old son and two-year-old daughter, said, "My identity was who I was when I worked. I had to reestablish a new identity. It took a good year to decide who I was and to feel comfortable with what I was doing."

When the shift does come, most mothers are pleased and more secure with the new version of themselves. One woman happily noted, "Now I'm *me* instead of my job title."

Some people adapt readily. They love the pattern and repetition, the intense intimacy, and the solitary refinement. Their inner clocks are quickly attuned to the rhythm of parenting. For these lucky souls, the shift to a self-image that reflects their role as mother may be all that is necessary.

The adaptation is not easy for everyone, though. In her book *Of Woman Born,* poet Adrienne Rich writes that mothers experience "not only physical, fleshy changes, but the feeling of a change in character. We learn, often through painful self-cauterization, those qualities which are supposed to be 'innate' in us: patience, self-sacrifice, the willingness to repeat endlessly the small, routine chores of socializing a human being. We are also, often to our amazement, flooded with feelings both of love and violence intenser and fiercer than any we have ever known."[10]

For many mothers, and especially for the numerous women whose successful experience in the work force has attuned them to the snappier rhythms and quantifiable achievements of shorter-term projects, adaptation may be especially difficult. But there is no reason why you should deny or sacrifice your desires, ambitions, and skills. To do so is to ignore all four of the ground rules.

Personal Growth: The Importance of a Room of Your Own

Most women do not want or need to become so dislocated that they lose the connection with their former self-concept. And make no mistake — there is a real danger here. The pervasive myth of the self-sacrificing mother, coupled with the very real demands placed on caretakers by young children and the repetition of work in the home, can undermine a woman's confidence in a life of her own and her sense of personal accomplishment.

Give yourself permission to have a life of your own: remember the ground rules. After all, pursuit of happiness is your inalienable right. It is not something you have to earn or bargain for with scraps of energy left over from your other roles and responsibilities.

Again and again, contemporary at-home mothers stress the importance of making time for themselves, for having, in Virginia Woolf's words, "a room of one's own" — a private, personal place, activity, or project that lets them define themselves; one that provides both the means to practice old skills and the opportunity to learn new ones. Not only does "the room" help you stay connected to your old identity, but it also gives you an arena in which to grow and develop mastery and self-esteem based on your new life.

Woolf used the term metaphorically, but we have found it useful as an actual conceptual tool. Try to imagine your "room." What is in it? It may be furnished with activities and connections to former or current roles, or it may act as an incubator for new endeavors. How do you like the balance of the decor? Just right? Too traditional? Too crowded with junk? Too many diapers, too few spreadsheets? An empty section over there in the creative corner? It's up to you to refurnish it.

Some women keep connected by doing free-lance work, keeping up with their professional associations and publications, continuing their education, or using their skills in volunteer or community organizations that can accommodate their children-first scheduling requirements and still provide opportunities to work on interesting projects. Those things would be in their rooms. Other women learn new sports, write articles, organize boycotts and fund-raisers, become experts on child development, make garments, start consulting businesses, do woodworking and crafts, remodel or decorate houses, or just set aside a quiet time to read or meditate. These things also furnish their rooms with richness and depth.

You can use your imaginary room as a self-esteem tool and identity check, mentally visiting it whenever you suspect that your self-concept is undergoing a particularly nasty assault. And remember, you can refurnish your room without knocking down any walls.

What surprises many women is how quickly their rooms fill up once their children are past the terribly demanding infant stage. Not only do they keep up their old skills, but they also develop new ones at a rate they couldn't have managed previously. *Indeed, opportunities for personal growth may be the best-kept secret about staying home.*

Pat Ricono, a credit analyst who is at home raising three sons, said, "I didn't lose my identity; it changed. I used my first year at home as an opportunity for things I always wanted to do but never had the time for when I was working, including exercise and nutrition. I have lost sixty pounds and have gotten in shape since I've been home! I'm back in school and look at myself more positively now. I've grown more in the six years I've been home than at any other time in my adult life."

Another at-home mother whose self-esteem and skills actually increased is a paralegal with two young daughters. She said, "I've become more competent since being a mother than I was when I was working. I know that whatever I set out to do, I can do. I'm now an officer of an nonprofit mothers' organization. Four years ago I never would have done it. I feel better about myself now. I know I can be a leader if I want to."

This growth may take place in several spheres: emotional, physical, intellectual, or creative. Looking back on how she has changed over her years at home, Victoria Harian Strella, previously an executive with the League of Women Voters and mother of a school-age son and a preschool daughter, said that "being an at-home mom has made me feel like a whole person, a real grown-up who is dependable and deeply loving, fully challenged both emotionally and intellectually (surprise!), and calmer and less anxiety-ridden than at any other time of my adult life. It has given me the chance to grow in ways that were unthinkable when my life was dominated by worries and stress over work, day care, commuting, weekends packed with endless chores, and life's daily monkey wrenches — sicknesses, car trouble, lost mittens, forgotten birthdays, and the rest."

One Woman Imagines Her Room

I have this imaginary room I visit when I want to get in touch with who I am. It looks a lot like the attic of my grandparents' beach house, which I used to visit in the summers. It's always mid-morning when I go up there — I can tell from the way the light comes in the window at the gable end. If I close my eyes, I can just hear the surf and catch a whiff of salt air.

This attic is full of trunks, shelves, and desks. Some of the trunks hold memories from high school and college, corsages and theater programs, degree certificates, the hospital ID bracelets from when my daughter, Sarah, was born, and imaginary photo albums full of fabulous pictures I would have taken if only I had had a camera at the right time.

Not all of the furnishings are memories of the past. A box of my watercolors sits on a desk, covered with a thin film of dust. I expect I'll get them out again someday, but for now I'm happy to know they're there — waiting for the day I come into the room with a fresh pad of rice paper. Piled on another desk are the newsletters from the programmers' society I still belong to. Sometimes I'm months behind on them, but it's good to know they're here if I need them. My jogging shoes are here, too. Unlike the watercolors, I feel a little guilty when I look at the shoes. Usually when I come up here, I tell myself that they really shouldn't be that dusty.

The messiest desk is this one here, under the window. It's covered with memos and reports from our local PTA. Two years ago this desk would have been empty, but when Sarah entered kindergarten, I started getting very interested in our local school system. In fact, this desk has so much overflow a lot of stuff has moved onto a bulletin board, like photos from class trips, six-year-old artwork from the refrigerator, and long lists of book reviews and recommendations.

An old egg crate filled with noxious chemicals, funny brushes, gloves, and a very expensive book on antique furniture restoration is tucked away in a corner of the attic, and as far as I'm concerned, it can stay there forever. The only reason I don't toss it out is that it serves to remind me that every new endeavor you try might not turn out to be for you — and that's certainly not a tragedy. In fact, the only tragedy would have been if I had kept on trying to convince myself that I enjoyed antiquing. And next to this egg crate is my old appointment book of tedious business dinners and meetings I used to have to attend. I guess I'm making a comment on both those endeavors by this placement!

And, of course, the room is littered with infant and child accessories — mismatched baby socks, well-loved stuffed animals, thousands of little Lego blocks, half-eaten Cheerios, and junk jewelry. Sometimes the mess gets on my nerves, but mostly I look at it fondly, remembering my daughter as I step over her artifacts. I suppose that soon I'll add to these her first makeup kit, algebra books, and maybe (but I hope not) a cheerleading outfit. I will always have more room in here for Sarah's mementos, as long as they don't completely cover up my image of myself.

My grandfather's old steamer trunk holds most of the artifacts that I associate with Jerry, my husband. There's everything here from old valentines and the lighting notes for the plays we used to put on together in college to the programs for some Broadway plays we saw during an outrageously expensive vacation we took right before Sarah was born. (We were right in assuming we wouldn't get away again for a *long* time!) There's also the huge, empty, economy-size bottle of stomach antacids he bought us when I was pregnant. Actually, we both ate them like candy. Thrown over the top of the trunk like a battle flag are several curiously shrunken cotton sweaters — mementos of Jerry's struggle to learn how to do laundry. One of the sweaters still carries a long, greasy stain — the result of my learning how to change the oil in the car. These are some of my favorite furnishings. I hope Jerry has them in his room, too.

The far wall of my room, the one with the window, is blank. At first this used to bother me. I took it as a rebuke, a failure to live a full life. Then one day I realized that of course it was blank; it was the future! Now when I come up here to visit, it is usually the last wall I look at. I imagine things I might like to be there five, ten, fifteen years from now. It's my favorite part of the visit.

6

Putting Your Marriage on a New Footing

My husband is one hundred percent supportive,
and I think that makes all the difference. He and I
feel that we share parenting responsibilities and that
each of us is contributing a necessary aspect of our
comfortable home life.
— Risa Scranton, *a mother who has been raising two
children at home for ten years*

When you change from a working woman to a full-time mother, you can expect to see some changes in your marriage. Just as you may have trouble giving up your old self-image as an independent wage earner, your husband may long for the good old days when you shared two professions — and two salaries. While you're busy constructing a new identity for yourself, you also have to think about redefining your roles within your family.

The transition to the home is easiest for couples when both husband and wife believe that having one parent stay home is best for the children. We found that the vast majority of the mothers we surveyed reported that their husbands were in favor of their staying home to raise their children. A surprising 73.3 percent of the women said that their husbands were either "somewhat" or "totally supportive"; less than 1 percent said that their husbands were "disapproving" (although 9.7 percent said that their husbands worried about money).

In many ways, a husband's emotional support for his wife is just as important as his financial support. Marnie Masterson told us, "From personal experience, from my job as a therapist and from feedback from other moms, I really feel that what makes or breaks one's experience as an at-home mom is the quality of one's marriage relationship. All of us have concerns and complaints regarding sleepless nights with infants or a child's adjustment to school, but it seems like those women who feel like they're part of a team in handling them cope most successfully." Knowing that your husband respects you and your new job at home can significantly cut down on the stress of those early days of at-home motherhood.

Unfortunately, not every new mother finds herself in that position. A technical writer remembers that although she and her husband expected that she would return to work after her daughter was born, she just could not stand the thought of leaving her baby. She told us, "I made as much money as my husband at that time, and we couldn't afford our house and car payments if I quit. That didn't matter to me. I was willing to give it all up to stay home with my baby. The problem was my husband. He didn't understand what had happened to me and to the dreams and plans we had shared. He insisted we could not afford for me to stay home, and I insisted I could not bear to leave my daughter."

This unexpected conflict caused a tremendous rift that resulted in the biggest crisis of their married life. After much discussion and several stormy fights, the woman went back to work after a three-month maternity leave. She quickly negotiated a compromise with her husband and her boss so that she could work three days a week. Eventually this mother was able to stay home when her daughter was fifteen months old and her husband changed jobs to earn a larger salary. She also arranged to do free-lance writing and editing at home for her employer.

Although their commitment to each other kept this couple's marriage intact, the conflict had long-lasting effects on their family life. She said sadly, "The resentment my husband felt toward me and our baby, which characterized most of her first year, still undermines their relationship almost six years later."

Many parents feel such a strong emotional attachment to their children that the work they used to do no longer matters as much. This attachment is not restricted to any one social class, career, or sex. It happens with lawyers and laborers, scientists and secretaries, mothers and fathers. Financial necessity may send them back to work, but the parents often find themselves losing interest in getting ahead as fast and may focus their energies on finding ways to maximize time with their child and keep one parent at home.

When both parents appreciate the other's attachment and agree about how it should be expressed, conflict over one parent staying home is usually minimal. However, if a woman longs to be at home and her husband is pressuring her to get back to work, she can feel betrayed and wonder whether he values her salary more than their child. Audrey Dittenberner told us, "I left my part-time sales job when my oldest child was four without support from my husband. He was shocked I couldn't be Superwoman anymore. The hardest thing for me about staying home was my husband not adjusting to the change and me not being able to do it all."

Even in the best of marriages, a husband can feel betrayed when the professional woman he married threatens to turn into a traditional full-time mother. When a woman gives up her career and decides to stay home, she is changing the rules of their marriage to date, and it's not surprising if her husband reacts with bafflement or anger. He admired her independence and enjoyed life as a double-income, no-kids family. When she suddenly gives that all up, he may feel "had" and wonder what happened to her belief in the equality of the sexes.

Having one partner stay home can be a good solution in healthy marriages, but it can be a mistake in troubled marriages or for couples who don't communicate well with each other. If you have trouble talking with each other now, if you can't get through daily conversations without arguing, or if you don't respect each other, trying to manage on a reduced income with new job descriptions can create more problems than it solves.

Being at odds over the decision for one parent to stay home can strain even the most solid marriage. To prevent this issue from becoming a major battleground, we suggest that you set aside some time to talk, without distractions, and ask each other these questions:

- What are our hopes for the family?
- How do we plan to achieve them?
- What is the value of each of our contributions to the family?
- Are we in desperate financial straits, or can we manage by careful budgeting?
- Can the working spouse stand the strain of being the sole provider?
- Is part-time work or work at home an option?
- *Her question for him:* Are you worried about the money, or are you worried that I'll change into a different person if I stay home?
- *His question for her:* How long are you planning to stay home — a year or two, until the children are grown, or until they enter school?

By taking the time to think about your priorities and the needs of the family and to discuss your feelings truthfully, you should start to understand each other's perspectives and take the first step toward a solution you can both live with.

Sometimes the passage of time will help you both get used to your career change. Susan M. Rathburn told us, "At first it was difficult for my husband because we had less money and he felt a lot of worry and pressure. During that period (almost the first three years I was home) there were a lot of tense times, but as time progresses my husband becomes more and more supportive and happy with the arrangement." Many women wrote that their husbands grew to value their work at home after seeing how happy and secure their children were.

Even those couples who never doubted the mother's decision to stay home can find those early months of parenthood rocky. Mothers aren't alone in finding it hard to get used to a baby. Fathers also may feel overwhelmed, exhausted, and uncertain about caring for a child, and they have the added weight of supporting the family financially. In addition, both parents may miss the intimate times they used to share. You may have enjoyed years of freedom together before the baby came along, and now you can't even have a conversation or private dinner without being interrupted by a crying infant with an insatiable appetite or smelly diaper. One couple asked, "Will our relationship ever be the same again? No matter how much we thought we were prepared for this, with a solid and tested marriage behind us, childbirth education, financial security and endless reading, the reality of having a newborn is inconceivable beforehand."[1]

As a new mother, you will probably struggle with trying to meet your baby's and your husband's needs at the same time. You may find that your husband feels neglected and needs extra attention and reassurance that he still matters to you. Unfortunately, there will be less time for the two of you. That's a fact of life when children come along. Having a baby is the beginning of your new life as a family. You're no longer just a couple, and your own needs no longer come first. This can lead to a feeling that your marriage is changing for the worse, or it can bring you a new sense of togetherness and a shared commitment to each other and your child.

Almost every couple goes through this period of adjustment, but there may be other strains on a marriage when the mother stays home. Your husband may not appreciate everything you do at home because he doesn't really know what you do all day. We heard from a number of women who said, "My husband doesn't realize how difficult my job is. He thinks it's all fun and games for me at home." One mother said, "My husband, who should be my staunchest supporter and ally, really has no grasp of the stress I deal with every day. I'm fully responsible for raising two children, caring for our home, and handling our finances. My husband still does not grasp that mine is a never-ending job."

You can help your husband learn more about your job if you borrow a method from the business world and do some cross-training. Your husband needs the opportunity to become familiar with and accomplished at baby care. If you're always responsible for those tasks, he won't be able to gain expertise at caring for his child or appreciate what's involved. (By the same token, if you never pay the bills or mow the lawn, you should learn how to perform these duties as well.) Until you take a day or weekend off regularly and leave him in charge, he may not realize how child care can expand to fill all your waking hours. An added benefit is that if you ever need to go out of town, return to work, or have a difficult pregnancy, your husband will know what to do, and your household will not fall apart.

Changing Financial Expectations

When you say good-bye to your former job and your paycheck, money can become an issue for the first time in your marriage. You may have been used to a comfortable life-style and been able to travel, buy expensive cars and other high-tech gadgets, and eat out a few times a week. Suddenly a large chunk of your income is gone, and you start thinking twice about the smallest purchases. A graphics designer said, "We used to spend endlessly and never balanced our checkbook for five years. It didn't matter: we just put more money in. Now we need to know the balance and be careful about what we spend." Money can be a constant source of stress and friction as you get used to having to make do with less.

Learning to live on one salary can be very hard. Cindy Emery spoke for a lot of at-home mothers when she said, "I resent people who say, 'You're lucky you can stay home.' They don't realize it isn't luck; it's hard work. We have sacrificed a lot. There are times when we don't know if we're going to make it — the mortgage payment, that is. No vacations, no new cars, no new clothes, juggling the bills, etc." Ironically, Cindy used to work as a manager of credit and collections.

In some ways, cutting down on your spending is like dieting. It's easier if you reconcile yourself to fewer indulgences but treat yourself to occasional splurges, then take as much pride in being able to live on a leaner salary as you might in having a leaner figure. Remember *Ground rule number 1: Know what you want your job to be.*

Managing on a Reduced Income

We asked the mothers in our survey for their experiences and advice on managing both emotionally and financially on a reduced income. Here are some of their comments.

- "It is hard to cope. There's so much we don't do or can't buy, and we've changed our eating habits. I do a lot of cooking from scratch. If you're staying home, it'd better be something you want to do. It's good to have friends in the same position; it's shared suffering. You don't feel so deprived."
- "The things I do aren't as expensive as [the things I used to do]. I don't have to worry about my wardrobe, commuting costs, and lunches out. I compare prices when grocery and clothes shopping. I save money by having more time. It's still difficult. But there are other values than material wealth. In the long run, we're doing fine."
- "It's surprising how much you can do without that you thought you had to have. You don't need to see the movie when it first comes out in the theater; you can get it on video later. We've deferred any materialistic feelings till someday."
- "We are renting a house instead of buying one. We've had the same car since 1983. I don't buy anything for myself. I make do with what I have."
- "We're both concerned about our finances: it's our common problem. We watch carefully what we spend. Before, if we wanted something, it was at our fingertips. We're in the process of looking for a new house now, and it's been shocking. We'd find it hard to afford our current house, let alone a new one."

- "Neither my husband nor I comes from a family that was materialistic. My parents were frugal, but we lived comfortably. I didn't have a lot of things as a kid, which has made it relatively easy now. There's not a lot of things where I think, 'I wish I were working so I could afford this.' "

- "When I resigned from my job, our family income decreased by forty-seven percent. We planned ahead by reducing our house payment, paying off the outstanding car loan, and reaching a comfortable amount in our savings. It was a leap of faith to go from two incomes to one and was not done without a few butterflies in the stomach. We are getting along so well now that we look back and wonder where all the money went before I quit my paying job."

- An eighty-six-year-old great-grandmother told us, "We started out very frugally, and we just couldn't have all the things that they do today. It seems like today children start out with what we worked all our lives for. We had to try to live within our means."

If you are committed to staying home and want this to be your job for the foreseeable future, that may help put the economies you make in perspective. They're making it possible for you to continue your chosen career. Living on a budget also may not be too much of a departure from what you were used to at work, as most professionals have to deal with budget constraints in the workplace.

For new parents who reached adulthood during the go-go 1980s, learning how to budget at home may be a new skill. It is one of the most valuable ones you can learn, though, as it can insulate your family from the boom-and-bust cycles of the general economy. Having a family standard of living based on quality of life, instead of material acquisition, is the only true measure of security.

It may comfort you to know that in making some financial sacrifices to stay home, you're in the forefront of a new social movement. A *Time* magazine cover story titled "The Simple Life" reports that Americans are turning away from the crass materialism and conspicuous consumption of the 1980s and are "embracing simpler pleasures and homier values." The story says that Americans are now thinking hard about what really matters in their lives and are choosing to spend more time with their families and less time at work. *Time* even proclaims that "penny pinching is back in vogue."[2] Now you can feel fashionable as well as fiscally responsible!

Some money-saving suggestions from the experienced at-home mothers we surveyed include growing your own vegetables; shopping in thrift stores and at garage sales; joining a food co-op, if you can find one locally; joining a baby-sitting co-op; looking for free family activities in the newspaper; washing your own cloth diapers; having "fiesta leftover" dinners; experimenting with vegetarian cooking. For more ideas, check out *The Heart Has Its Own Reasons* by Mary Ann Cahill. This La Leche League International publication offers 340 pages of advice on saving and earning money at home.

Some mothers are ashamed about having to live frugally and not being able to buy their children the latest "must-have" toys or the most fashionable clothes. You may feel that by choosing to stay home, you're losing status and coming down in the world. If you're feeling unhappy or bitter about the lack of money, remember that millions of other American families are in the same situation. Heidi L. Brennan, codirector of Mothers at Home, said, "You're not the only one being frugal, although it may look that way. Many of us have pretty tight financial circumstances. That's the worst part — feeling you're the only one clipping coupons. You'd be surprised how many people are doing that."

While not having enough money can be stressful, it's often not the real reason couples find themselves quarreling over finances. Many mothers who have left the work force are surprised to discover how much of their identity and self-respect are wrapped up in their earning power. Joan Torkildson, a free-lance copy editor, said, "I think it took two or three years of being an at-home mother before I began to feel comfortable with my career choice. In the beginning I wrestled with guilt over not contributing financially, even though I was working harder and longer hours than ever before." It may take you quite a while before you learn to value your other contributions to the family instead of worrying about the money you aren't earning.

While you are coming to terms with this issue, your husband may find it stressful to be solely responsible for the family's standard of living. He may feel so much pressure to succeed at work that he starts staying at the office late every night and risks becoming a workaholic. He may have to stay in a boring job he doesn't enjoy because it's secure and pays well instead of taking a risk of finding something else. Or he may have to work two jobs to meet the family's expenses. He may even feel like a failure if the family is finding it hard to live on what he earns.

A reference librarian told us, "A side effect of my decision to stay home was one I had never anticipated: my husband started questioning his worth as a provider! He began wondering, 'I have a Ph.D., I have nine years' experience, and I don't make enough money to support my wife and daughter for even a couple of years? What is wrong here? What is wrong with me?' "

As many men have pointed out, women whose financial situations enable them to stay home are fortunate in having the freedom to decide whether or not to return to work. Although a small number of men are beginning to experience at-home fatherhood, most men don't have the luxury of making that choice. They are simply expected to take up the burden of supporting their family.

Victor C. Larson, an Illinois father who takes his family life and work responsibilities seriously, said, "I find it extremely frustrating to overhear discussions among women who complain bitterly about their 'lot in life' and the 'easy escape' that men with new children enjoy. I have never pretended for a moment that my wife does not have a difficult job ahead of her raising our children. But I have a difficult job as well, and we each experience different sets of pressures and responsibilities."[3]

Your husband also may worry about how he can be both successful in his career and an active, involved father. Ann Cocks, a former promotion manager at home with two children, reminded us that "when husbands are working hard to advance in their careers and women are at home with young children, this is a stressful time for both sides of the equation. It is easy for both mothers and fathers to feel beleaguered, unsupported, and unappreciated. Recognizing and accepting this factor can avoid fights, though not, perhaps, some of the frustrations."

It helps to keep in mind *Ground rule number 3: Validate yourself* and apply it to your husband. He needs your support and encouragement as much as you need his. Remember to tell him how much you appreciate all the work he does for the family and how lucky you feel to be able to stay home with your children. Let him know that he can count on you, too, and that if your financial situation deteriorates drastically, you will do what you can to earn money to keep the family afloat — either by finding ways to make money at home or returning to outside employment. It may not alleviate all his fears, but it will help him to know that you're on his side and value his efforts.

Dealing with Feelings of Dependency

Losing financial independence and a hard-won sense of autonomy are major problems for career women who become at-home mothers. The fear of being abandoned and becoming a "displaced homemaker" (a woman who is left impoverished and jobless after a divorce) in later life is a real one, and a woman can feel very vulnerable as an at-home mother of preschool children. This fear of dependency can drive many at-home mothers back to work and can prevent some from allowing themselves to stay home in the first place. Women who were taught by the feminist movement of the sixties and seventies that housewives are an oppressed minority who should be earning their own living and yet long to be full-time mothers can find themselves in a real dilemma.

The dependency issue is probably at the root of any tensions or arguments you and your husband have about your financial situation. Whose money is it, anyway? Who's in charge here? Being dependent on your husband's income can upset the balance of a marriage used to financial equality. According to Lynne Hofer, a psychotherapist and research associate at Cornell University, "Today, it takes a strong marriage for people to live on one income. Often it's not just a question of whether there is really enough money for young couples to live on, but rather who has control over that money. So many women have told me that they don't want to be like their own mothers."[4]

If you were used to spending your own money on anything you chose and had an equal voice in your joint purchasing decisions, you may feel resentful and powerless if that freedom is taken away from you now that you're at home. A probation officer who left her job to stay home with her children describes a worst case scenario: "I don't like being financially dependent on my husband and at his mercy. He puts his paycheck into an account that only he has access to, and he allocates money to me to pay the bills and buy groceries. I find it very demeaning that he doesn't trust me with a joint account, particularly since I've always been very frugal. This is one of the problems with our marriage, and I do not foresee our marriage lasting 'until death do us part.'"

The women we interviewed who received a weekly allowance and had to justify every penny they spent to their husbands were the most frustrated. A special education teacher told us about her struggles with this issue in her marriage: "I always feel dependent as an at-home mother. It can really damage your self-esteem. You can feel like a little girl going to Daddy and saying, 'Please, can I get this?' I really don't think of the money as ours. We're trying to remedy that with separate checking accounts. It's humiliating: whoever has the money has the power in a relationship."

An unequal balance of power can affect other aspects of your marriage, so it's best to prevent it from happening even before you stay home. When you and your husband sit down to make your budget, you might want to think about the going rate for child care and household work. As we mentioned in Chapter 4, that figure is approximately $52,000 a year, depending on where you live. By putting a value on the work you do as a mother and home manager, you will be less likely to be treated as a nonproductive member of your household. Joyce Holte, a college professor on a one-year maternity leave, said that she does not feel dependent on her husband because "I'm working just as hard here in the house, earning our money in a different way. I may be dependent on his salary — that's the reality — but I don't perceive it that way."

A number of women in our survey found this solution: they share monetary responsibilities with their husband by being in charge of the family's finances. By dividing up the work this way, you'll continue to be an important part of the family's financial decision making. The goal is to find ways for you and your husband to take a team approach and depend on each other rather than having someone be the boss. It *is* possible to live in a "traditional family" while preserving the equality and mutual respect of the best modern marriages.

An article in *New Woman* magazine offers some additional suggestions for couples facing this issue:

> Think of your new full-time role as a regular job and the money your husband will spend on your support as a salary — i.e. you're earning it. (Never call yourself "financially dependent," which connotes that you're getting a free ride!) Next, implement financial systems that show you're working to earn your way, albeit at home.
>
> • Try not to ask your husband for money. Establish a joint checking account, have his paycheck deposited in it, and pay bills yourself out of that account.
> • Avoid having your husband give you a lump sum each month to pay the bills. This system can make you feel like the "child" being given an "allowance."
> • Before the baby arrives, agree to hire a baby-sitter at regular intervals so you can have a break. After all, other workers get time off.
> • Keep in mind that what you're dividing is the labor, not the power, in your family. If your husband treats you differently because you're home full-time, gently remind him that if you weren't taking care of the kids, he would have to — or pay for child care.[5]

From "Money Matters" by Claudia Bowe, August 1991. Reprinted by permission from *New Woman*.

That said, some women are not happy until they are earning some money themselves, even if it's much less than their old salary. Many of the women we surveyed have developed some way to earn income at home, whether it's doing free-lance writing or editing, selling crafts, working part-time during school hours, doing day care in their home, acting as a consultant to small businesses, selling Tupperware, or applying other work skills. For some families, this extra money is necessary to make it possible for one parent to stay home. Other women have an emotional need to continue earning money, even though the financial need may not be there.

Jacqueline Steltz-Lenarsky, who lives in southern California, told us, "I do feel dependent, and that bothers me. Almost all the women I know are working, and I feel like a kept woman." Jacqueline is a talented musician and recently recorded a flute track for a friend's upcoming jazz album. She said, "I did that and didn't think much about it. Later, I was surprised to get a check for $100 in the mail. It was the first check I'd earned in four years, and it felt wonderful. There is something about earning it yourself." If you also feel this way about money, you probably will be more comfortable about being home if you can find ways to earn income of your own, whether or not your family finances require it.

Staying active in your field of expertise can help both of you worry less about what would happen to your family if your husband was laid off or disabled or if you got divorced and needed to reenter the job market quickly. One woman who is working one day a week at a management-level marketing position said she's not concerned about being dependent because she knows she could always go back to work full-time and become the primary wage earner if her husband lost his job. If you aren't currently working for pay, remember that you built up a career before you stayed home and that you are fully capable of earning your own living. You won't be in a dependent position forever, so there's no reason to be apologetic about leaving your previous work to take on the important job of raising your children.

Sex Role Stereotypes and the Division of Labor

Marital expectations, both spoken and unspoken, can radically change once a woman decides to stay home. You may have enjoyed an equal relationship before, but once you give up your position outside the home, it can be a whole new ball game with a new set of rules. Many couples find themselves slipping into the same old sex role stereotypes that they grew up with — the husband as the breadwinner, whose work stops as soon as he walks in the door at night; the wife as the bread baker, whose work involves everything that needs to be done for the children and the house.

This change can be shocking for women who considered their husbands to be fairly liberated in their prechildren days. A registered nurse said that the hardest part about being home is "my husband's antiquated idea about roles and the feeling of being a downtrodden housewife." You may find that you both become more locked into traditional roles and that your husband is unwilling to help with home chores and child care because he sees them as your responsibility. Some at-home mothers contribute to this problem by believing that they are the experts at child care and housework and that no one else can do them as well. By holding this belief, they may discourage their husbands from even trying to help. Women who feel dumped on can internalize a lot of resentment, anger, and jealousy of their husbands' freedom and free time. After financial pressures, these role conflicts and the unequal distribution of household burdens are the most common problems couples face.

No discussion of your new relationship with your partner can proceed very far without dealing with one of the biggest bugaboos: housework. Fear of becoming a household drudge is one of the fears most often mentioned by the women in our survey. The division of household chores when one parent is at home can be especially problematic for husbands and wives who have worked hard to achieve a partnership marriage and like to think of themselves as a modern, feminist couple.

In fact, the division of household chores can be an issue for families no matter how many members are in the outside work force.[6] And no matter whether we honor it or not, housework is a dominant social activity. It is usually the first form of work we experience as children and the only form of work that each of us — male and female, adult and child — pursues for at least some portion of every week. It is also the occupational category that encompasses the single largest fraction of our population: full-time homemakers (who may or may not have children at home).

Despite this universality, there is no doubt that the nature of housework changes radically when children come into the home. Laundry and cleaning tasks rise exponentially, a whole new range of products must be shopped for and maintained, and cooking and feeding become more complicated. This doesn't include the care of the children who, whether they are being bathed, fed, dressed, played with, nursed, rocked to sleep, read to, or just cuddled, must be attended to.

How is the division of chores, both old and new, to take place? Some women, especially if they are feeling guilty about giving up their former careers or putting too much financial burden on their husbands, may offer to take on the entire running of the household themselves — and their husbands are usually quick to accept. Several months later, after an unremitting stream of fourteen-hour days and seven-day workweeks, the women may come to regret this offer.

A popular misconception of the twentieth century has been that modern technology has so radically transformed the American household that housework, while boring, is minimal in terms of the energy and time expended. This is simply not so.

Ironically, while modern laborsaving devices such as the stove, plumbing, microwave oven, and washing machine save labor, the labor they save is not that of the average housewife, but of the husband and children. In her famous study of household labor, *More Work for Mother,* historian Ruth Schwartz Cowan traced the industrialization of the American household from the eighteenth century to modern times. She found that if you had been a homemaker before 1800, you would have spent a good part of your workday cooking and baking, but your husband would have participated in much of the preparation by chopping wood, shelling corn, and pounding grain into meal. Your children would have helped as well, fetching wood and water and taking care of the domestic animals.

With the coming of industrialization, more and more households had stoves and plumbing and used store-bought flour and cloth. But Cowan found that most devices replaced men's traditional household chores, such as chopping wood and pounding grain, and freed them for work in factories or mills outside of the home. Children, who traditionally performed chores such as hauling water and carding wool, were freed to attend school. But the women still cooked and cleaned, and as standards of hygiene and diet rose, these chores actually increased, instead of decreased. Ironically, this rise in the quality of life standards also meant that just as men's share in domestic activity began to decrease, women's increased. Thus, for the first time housework was becoming truly "women's work" and not an obligation to the homestead shared by both sexes.

As industrialization increased, so did traditionally female chores. For example, laundry is so arduous a task that laundresses were once the most numerous of all specialized house servants. Many women who did their own cooking, sewing, and cleaning would have a laundress in to do the wash or send the heavy washing out to be done. The development of the electric washing machine in the twentieth century coincided with the advent of do-it-yourself laundries, so the woman endowed with a washer would have found it easier to do her laundry. Simultaneously, however, she would be doing more laundry, and more of it herself without any help, than either her mother or her grandmother. The amount of laundry continued to increase, as a daily change of clothes and clean sheets every week became the norm. Today the amount of laundry the average family generates, with work clothes, casual clothes, gym clothes, and an unlimited supply of fresh bedding and towels, would be inconceivable even to a wealthy nineteenth-century matron.[7]

We are not saying that machines don't save time. It is irrefutable that they do. However, they save so much time that they eliminate worker positions — workers who used to help the homemaker run her household. The typical nineteenth-century middle-class household ran on the labor of four to six people: nurse or nanny, cook, laundress, maids, gardener, and stable boy. Today a typical middle-class household runs on the labor of one or two people.

Another interesting change in household technology is that in earlier times all manner of goods and services came right to the homemaker's door. Peddlers carried cloth and pots and pans, the greengrocer's wagon delivered vegetables, and pushcarts brought goods right to your curb. Laundry could be picked up and delivered, the seamstress came to your house, and even doctors made house calls. It was so unusual for housewives to have to do their own procurement that among retailers the term *carriage trade* came to signify only the richest clientele — those who could afford to send their own carriage (and a servant) to pick up goods.

As the suburbs continue to spread and neighborhood stores disappear, today's housewife is hard-pressed to run a household without a car, performing for her family herself the numerous services that retailers, servants, and professionals once did. One at-home mother from California with two school-age sons, pausing to reflect on her life in between seemingly unremitting rounds of laundry, cooking, cleaning, shopping, and chauffeuring, said "My God, my life has become a service industry!" The combination of industrialization, suburban expansion, and universal education can result in a situation where the house becomes a place of leisure and renewal for your husband and children, while for you it is a source of endless work and little pleasure.

Some women are sincerely interested in the domestic arts and welcome the chance to expand their interests in areas such as cooking and sewing. Even for those who enjoy these pursuits, however, the entire burden of housework is too heavy. In her book *Family Politics,* Letty Cottin Pogrebin reports that only about one in ten husbands share housework. She found that women at home spend eight hours and forty-two minutes daily on house and family work; employed women spend five hours. Men and children combined spend just one and a half hours each day on housework.[8]

111

In *The Second Shift,* a much-talked-about study of work on the home front, sociologist Arlie Hochschild argues that women who work outside the home also struggle with an inequitable distribution of household tasks in their families. Hochschild commented, "Just as there is a wage gap between men and women in the workplace, there is a leisure gap between them at home."[9] The majority of men in her survey did not share the load at home, and those who did do some of the housework avoided daily tasks such as cooking dinner and undesirable chores such as scrubbing the bathroom.

A recent article in London's *Daily Mail* reported similar figures on how husbands and wives across the Atlantic handle domestic chores. Asking "Who does what at home?" the pollsters found that 77 percent of British women cook the evening meal each night, 72 percent do all the household cleaning, 88 percent do all the washing and ironing, and 50 percent do all the household shopping. By contrast, 83 percent of the men do all the household repairs.[10] Again, most of the women's chores must be done daily, while the men's chores are done less often and can be scheduled at a convenient time.

The bad news is that this situation does not seem to be changing, despite the gains of the women's movement. Not surprisingly, marital conflict can increase when the partners disagree about allocating household work. One at-home mother admits that her decision to stay home initially made her husband somewhat resentful and that now she does more for him, such as doing his laundry and ironing — things he used to do for himself when they were a two-career couple. Even though her husband performs fewer household chores than he used to, this woman doesn't consider it a problem, since she considers "caring for the children and the house" to be her full-time job. Other couples talk about the team approach, in which husband and wife are parts of a team with different tasks.

Couples should take a long, hard look at their division of labor to see what sort of model they are providing for their children. We found that many mothers worry that their children might grow up to share society's stereotyped view that housework is woman's work. One mother in our survey said, "I recently came to the realization that it's useless to clean or pick up all day when I had a discussion with my four-year-old. I asked him, 'What kind of things does Mommy do for fun? What makes Mommy happy?' He said, 'Washing dishes.' His words hit me like a hammer on my head. I don't want him to think I'm into housework for fulfillment! What kind of a role model is that?"

Couples who want to avoid this problem should ask themselves these questions:

- Have we divided up the tasks according to individual talents and likes and dislikes, or automatically according to gender?
- Does the home-and-children job run from 7 A.M. to 10 P.M. six or seven days a week, while the office job only lasts from 9 A.M. to 6 P.M. five days a week?
- Do both jobs get days off, downtime, relief?

Unless your family is in the financial position to buy a lot of services, chores must be divided sensibly between mother and father. If the household chores last until nine or ten at night — and in many households with young children they do, since parents are concerned with child care for so much of the children's waking time — shouldn't it be just as easy for the father as for the mother to throw a load of laundry into the washer or fold towels? Of course, he has been working all day — but so has she! It is also just as easy for the mother to cut the grass or wash the family car now and then instead of leaving it all for her husband to do.

If you had previously been sharing chores as a dual-career couple, your staying at home need not become an automatic signal for your husband to retreat from all domestic endeavors. His participation is needed even more now because the work load at home has increased dramatically.

As we mentioned in Chapter 3, fathers are a vital part of an at-home mother's support network. Full-time mothers need both practical and emotional support to fulfill household and child-care responsibilities without burning themselves out. If the mother is the relief parent for the father at work, the father has to realize that he is the relief worker for the mother at home.

Strategies for Delegating Household Chores

Let's look at some of your options in negotiating these issues. First of all, remember that you can decide what you want your job to be. If you don't enjoy domestic life and are staying home because you want to provide high-quality care for your children, not for your house, don't let housework dominate your life. Housework has to be done eventually, but it doesn't have to take up all your free time. You can escape the stereotype of the happy homemaker by making it clear to your husband and your family what you consider your role as an at-home mother to be and by doing some problem solving together to find ways to share the load. After all, you didn't leave a fulfilling job in the work force to stay home and scrub floors.

You can start to resolve this by sitting down with your husband and listing everything that needs to be done at home and then deciding together which chores are urgent, which need to be done regularly, and which you can safely ignore. After all, a dust-ball collection under the furniture is probably not going to endanger your children's health or cause the house to fall down. After that, draw up a chart and figure out who will be in charge of recurring tasks such as washing dishes, doing laundry, vacuuming, shopping for food, scrubbing the toilet (a particularly sticky issue), taking care of the yard, taking out the garbage, and doing household repairs. If you calculate how much time each of these tasks takes each week, these figures may help to convince your husband that you can't do them alone.

Each husband and wife need to come to their own decision about how to share the work involved in maintaining a home and raising a family. For example, a mother at home with two preschoolers and an infant is going to need a lot more participation from her husband than a mother whose children are in school all day. What is important is that you both agree to take responsibility for your assigned chores instead of your having to nag him to do his part. Christine Davidson writes in *Staying Home Instead,* "Husbands sometimes 'help' with the housework or 'baby-sit' the children in the evenings, but many still do not share responsibility, and there is a

114

big difference. Fixing the sink or mowing the lawn once a week doesn't make up for the disparity."[11]

In dividing up the household work, some couples prefer to alternate weeks in doing chores such as vacuuming and cleaning the bathroom; others prefer to specialize by, for example, having one partner cook and the other one clean up. It's a good idea to put all this in writing to save arguments later over who promised to do what. You might want to reevaluate this list periodically and switch chores at times to make them seem less tedious.

What if your husband doesn't respond to this rational approach to the division of labor? Some husbands feel that they do their work five days a week in the office and shouldn't have to work at home, too. How can you make him understand that you are working seven days a week and perhaps get to an equitable situation where you both work a six-day week, providing relief for each other? Some mothers swear by the indirect method. Pat Ricono, a mother of three young boys, told us how she handles housework she doesn't want to do. "My husband does all the vacuuming, when the dirt on the carpet starts to mount up. There are certain things I ignore, like the windows. When they get bad enough, he takes care of them."

At this point, some of you might be thinking, "This idea of sharing the load is great in principle, but my husband travels and works late most of the time and just isn't around to do his part." You can pursue other solutions without having to resign yourself to being a full-time maid. As your children get older, you can assign them chores such as setting the table and dusting, then have them graduate to sorting clothes or cleaning their own room. You will probably spend more time showing your kids how to do the chores and reminding them to complete them than if you did the work yourself, but it will teach them that their participation is necessary to keep the family running smoothly.

In an ideal world, you could hire someone to handle the cleaning chores so you could concentrate on raising your children. One mother of two daughters who works one day a week uses part of the income she brings home to have a cleaning service come in every other week. She told us, "We also have someone cut our grass. We use outside services a lot. I'd rather work a few more hours and pay someone else to clean my house than to do it myself and be very aggravated." If your budget does not allow you to hire a professional cleaning service, you might be able to find a high school or college student to come in for a few hours at a much more reasonable rate.

Another option is to relax your standards and decide that you don't have to be the perfect TV mother or have the cleanest house in the neighborhood. For example, there's no rule that you have to cook dinner from scratch every night. If your husband comes home too late during the week to take part in cooking dinner, why not institute a pizza night (or Chinese or Mexican carryout, if you prefer) to give yourself a break? Or you can plan weekend cooking marathons where the whole family helps make up frozen dinners for the rest of the week. Linda Lewis Griffith advises, "Give yourself permission to have a less-than-perfect life. Your windows needn't be spotless, and your dinners don't have to be gourmet. What is important is that you are providing a loving environment for your family and making time for your own needs as well as theirs."[12]

By making an effort to divide up household work fairly and to avoid being trapped by old sex role stereotypes, you may end up effecting societal change. A California mother at home offers a good example of *Ground rule number 4: Consider yourself a feminist* in action. She said that she and her husband are working hard to ensure that they don't raise another generation of sexists. They have decided that her daytime job is raising her daughter — period. Their daughter learns about household chores through both of them; she shares in grocery shopping with her father and folds laundry with her mother. This mother believes that couples who have more traditional roles still owe it to their children to break out of the molds periodically.[13]

Are Sex and Intimacy Possible After Childbirth?

When we asked the women in our survey, "What effect has becoming an at-home mother had on your marriage?" we found a real diversity of opinions. Many women reported this paradox: having children has made their marriage better, but they regret having less time for intimacy and communication.

Thirty-eight percent of our survey respondents said that their marriage is now stronger than it was before children, and an additional 15.5 percent said that they feel less tense with each other. One mother explained why she feels her marriage has improved since she has been home: "Before our child was born, I can see now that my husband and I led sort of parallel lives. We lived together peaceably, but we were really more involved in our jobs than with each other. Now my husband takes more of an interest in me and in our child, and I think about my relationship with him and how to improve it much more than I have in years."

This good news is balanced by those 14.6 percent who said that their marriage has become more strained since children came along. Never having enough time alone together was cited most often as the major problem, along with issues such as disagreements about how to raise the children, feeling that the romance has gone out of their marriage, and feeling unappreciated by their partner. Other couples find that the more their child starts to communicate, the less they communicate with each other. This bleak picture was painted by a twenty-six-year-old mother who is also a home day-care provider: "My husband and I never talk now. We don't have fun anymore. He comes home late usually, and my son and I have already eaten. We do chores all evening, and then at eleven o'clock we go to bed — to sleep. Our marriage is much worse than before our child was born. And now I don't even have time to care about it."

To prevent this from happening in your marriage, consider one solution many experienced at-home mothers swear by: making regular dates with their husbands a top priority. These couples have a standing appointment with a baby-sitter who comes one night a week, and they use that time to take a walk, go out to a movie or a coffee shop, and catch up on each other's lives without interruption. Making time for intimate conversations can be invaluable in maintaining your closeness, instead of feeling that your change of jobs means that you're now on different wavelengths. If you can't afford to or can't find time for one date a week, try once or twice a month.

If that's not possible, try setting early bedtimes for your children and use that time for each other. A teacher told us that she and her husband make sure their three children are in bed by eight or eight-thirty so they can have the whole evening to themselves. She commented, "Early bedtime for our kids is key for us. We wouldn't have a marriage without it."

Another common problem, which is not so easily solved, revolves around sex. There usually isn't much time for it with young children around, and many mothers experience reduced sexual desire for quite a while after their babies are born. Some fathers also are less interested in sex after being present during labor and child birth. A *Parenting* magazine study of nearly 6,000 readers found that many new parents go into a sexual hiatus that lasts for at least a year. The main reasons the couples they surveyed had sex less often were fatigue and lack of desire.[14]

Another reason sex becomes less frequent is that full-time mothers often find their emotional needs met through nursing and caring for their children all day. They no longer have to rely on their husbands as the only source of intimacy and comfort. Many mothers are so tired of holding a child all day that the last thing they want when their husbands come home is more physical contact. *Parenting* found that 91 percent of the women and 83 percent of the men surveyed agree that the mother of a young child often pays more attention to the baby than to her husband.[15]

This can be hard for husbands to understand. They are often frustrated and take it personally when their wives aren't interested in sex for weeks or months at a time. One father of two children who took part in a *Parenting* survey on father's attitudes toward sex said, "With the arrival of our first baby, our sex life plummeted, and it's never quite gotten back to normal. After our baby was born, we had seven months without sex. The frustration nearly brought me to the breaking point. I was incredibly angry because I wasn't being accepted by my wife."[16]

Some couples never go back to having sex as frequently as they did in the early stages of their marriage, but they usually find that their sex life picks up as their children leave the infancy stage. In some ways, having sex less often can make it more romantic and exciting when it does occur.

Although the following suggestions may not be for every couple, the mothers in our survey proposed these innovative solutions for making time for sex as busy parents. Arranging a weekend getaway every now and then without children is the best solution for maintaining that spark in your sex life. You don't need to go far from home; look for good weekend rates at nearby hotels. If that's not financially possible, consider a rendezvous at home behind closed doors whenever the opportunity arises. One woman said that she and her husband swear by their "basement escapes" when the kids are busy watching "Sesame Street."

Or you might recapture your teenage years and go parking or take in a drive-in movie. Don't overlook the possibility of making love during your child's nap time or climbing into the shower together on the weekend. If you're feeling desperate, you could even hire a baby-sitter and go to a local motel for the evening instead of going out for dinner and a movie. When children are older, sending them off to slumber parties can give you a welcome opportunity for sexual intimacy without interruptions.

Sometimes energy, and not interruptions, is the problem. After a full day of running after the children or trying to get a product ready to ship, sex and intimacy may be the last thing on your or your husband's mind. At these times, it's important not to give up on intimacy just because it may not lead to sex. Having him scrub your back in the tub or exchanging neck and foot rubs on the couch, as well as making time for copious cuddles, can help couples keep in touch with each other for the full range of physical and emotional communication.

Sex counselor Cindy Power recommends, "Arrange with your partner to spend time *alone together* every week — not necessarily to have sex, but rather just to be together. Then if lovemaking happens, you may find you're *both* in the mood. Remember, having a plan doesn't destroy spontaneity; it creates opportunity."[17]

Fortunately, not every couple experiences a disappointing decline in their sex life after they have children. A few of our survey respondents said that they have sex more often now that they're at home because they are no longer as stressed and depleted as they were after a hard day at the office.

Although most couples experience some marital tensions with the birth of a child, many husbands and wives report that they have never felt closer to each other. At-home mothers, in particular, are able to nurture their family life instead of focusing on a work-oriented life-style. One woman told us, "Before we had our child, our lives revolved around work and our schedule was always frantic. Now, although we are still busy, we have a sense of shared identity and a true home life."

All relationships are different, and not every issue discussed in this chapter will apply to yours. Paying attention to the coping strategies we've outlined here, however, should help you resolve some of the tensions you or your husband may be feeling and enrich your marriage.

7

Changing Relationships with Others

Since I had children, my mother and I finally have
something we can talk about without arguing!
— Kim Cook, *registered nurse and at-home mother*

Family

A woman's relationship with her spouse is not the only one to
undergo significant changes when she becomes an at-home mother.
Relationships with friends, colleagues, and other family members
also change.

Your family and friends can be a microcosm of all the issues
and conflicts about at-home mothering in society at large. You may
encounter the full range of reactions — from total support to total
rejection, and everything in between. The difference is that because
you have closer relationships with family and friends, the feelings
will be more intense and complex.

While first-time mothers experience a new depth in their relationship with their own mothers, at-home mothers may experience an additional emotional dimension. Career-minded baby
boomers who previously felt superior to their own fifties-style mothers may develop a new appreciation of just how much time, effort,
skill, and energy those women put into raising them.

"I never realized it before," one at-home mother of two said, "but I never used to have a lot of respect for what my mother did with her life. Now that I'm home with my boys, my whole attitude has changed. I mean, I always loved her, but now I respect her, too. And I'm sure she can feel the new warmth in our relationship." More than 38 percent of the at-home mothers in our survey reported that their choice has made their relationship with their own mothers stronger; only 7.5 percent indicated that the relationship was "more strained."

Although full-time parenting can make women appreciate their own mothers more, they may not be as appreciative of their mothers' homemaker expectations. As we have shown, contemporary at-home mothers do not make an automatic link between housework and child care — a connection that their parents' generation may have taken for granted. One grandmother of two expressed her disappointment at the condition of her daughter's house, which she felt should be in tip-top, *House Beautiful* condition now that her daughter was no longer going to the office ten hours a day. Little did she realize that between play group, exercise class, and library board meetings, her daughter was rarely home ten hours a day in her new full-time job as mother, either. And even if she was home, she usually spent her free time reading, not dusting. Even grandmothers can suffer from motherhood misconceptions.

Motherhood misconceptions from other family members can be especially hurtful when they interfere with your family's adherence to the ground rules. For example, one couple had decided to enroll their three-year-old daughter in a local preschool. They felt that a few mornings a week might be fun for her and give her more children to play with, a chance to develop group social skills, and a wider variety of activities than at home. This couple also had a one-year-old son, so the mother was looking forward to being able to devote some more attention to him, in addition to getting (after three years of intensive child care) a little break for herself.

Both sets of grandparents were highly critical — but only of the woman. "Why," they challenged, "did you quit your high-paying job to stay home with the children if you are only going to send them away?" Obviously, these grandparents' definition of the mothering job was twenty-six hours a day with no breaks — a definition that did not agree with this particular couple's definition, which included the ability to delegate and the right to time off.

Even worse, the grandparents implied that this woman was putting an unnecessary burden on her husband by making him the sole breadwinner and then "spending *his* good money for someone else to look after the child." This type of challenge to a woman's self-esteem can be especially hurtful when it comes from someone she loves. In this woman's case, even though she and her husband were in agreement, she had to seek additional support and advice from her mothers' group to deal with the attack.[1]

In some cases, jealousy or pride can interfere with your loved ones' ability to recognize and honor your choice. A thirty-six-year-old attorney with two children says that some family members keep asking her why she went to law school if she was "only going to stay home with the kids." This woman is resigned to having to remind them that "just because I'm an attorney doesn't mean that that is more important to me than raising my kids."

Many other women mention subtle shifts in their status in the family: their opinions are solicited less frequently or dismissed when offered, their housekeeping and child-care standards are criticized more often, and they may even be inundated with requests to run errands or perform services for other family members "now that you have so much free time." Cathy Bendzunas related this experience: "After working for so many years, I had a lot of conflicting feelings about staying home. I felt it was best for my children, but it seemed like everyone else in my family thought I was being lazy, worthless, and sponging off my husband instead of paying my fair share."

Although attacks like this can occur, most women find that the family atmosphere is overwhelmingly positive. More than 70 percent of the mothers surveyed reported that their decision to stay home with their children was "totally supported" by their families, and 17.7 percent reported a "somewhat supportive" response. Many women told us that their mother and mother-in-law had stayed home to raise their children, and were delighted that they chose to do the same.

Unfortunately, having a mother who stayed home doesn't guarantee that she will approve of your choice. A special education teacher said, "A great disappointment has been my mother, who was unhappy as an at-home mother as part of a generation with few options. She assumed that all three of her daughters would launch into full-fledged careers given the opportunities she lacked. Both my parents seem to wonder if I am wasting my education — and their support of my education."

In our survey 2 percent of the women reported a disapproving reaction from their families, while 1.5 percent reported some jealousy on the part of other family members. Even those who have experienced disapproval are aware that the negative reaction often can come from true concern. One displaced homemaker grandmother, left impoverished after a bitter divorce, counseled her at-home daughter to keep working so that she could remain financially independent. The daughter appreciates her mother's concern but as a nurse feels that reentry into the job market would not be a problem should the need arise.

As we've seen in this chapter, the same motherhood mythology and assumptions that affect the population at large can undermine your vision of yourself as a full-time parent and can harm your relationship with your family. Try to apply the ground rules set forth in Chapter 3 and don't let the extra emotion you bring to these encounters undermine your resolve.

Friends and Colleagues

While relationships with family members usually grow closer, many at-home mothers report difficulty maintaining their relationships with childless friends and office colleagues. *All* new parents notice a drifting away of childless friends as concerns and schedules change, but isolated at-home mothers may feel these losses more keenly, especially if they are trying to keep up professional relationships with an eye to the future.

If you want to maintain these relationships, you can, but it will take extra effort on your part. For example, former friends are often more separated by time than temperament. They may visit the same places: grocery store, library, health club, shopping center, post office, movie theater, and so on, but women who work in offices tend to be in these places after 5 P.M., while full-time mothers tend to be there in the morning or afternoon. Socializing, shopping, and exercising — activities that formerly took place in the evening — can no longer be shared, and the gulf between friends gradually widens. And without the reinforcement of daily contact that work provides, office relationships can wither away even more quickly.

At-home mothers who want to keep up with their former friends and colleagues must be willing to make special arrangements and go to a little extra trouble to keep in touch. Cards and a schedule of weekly calls help to keep you connected so that when you do get together, you're still up-to-date with one another. If there is a company newsletter, the at-home mother should make sure she continues to receive it.

How friends get together also is important. One mother was very successful in keeping up with her office friends by maintaining her membership in the health club they all belonged to. She made a point of visiting the club in the evenings or on weekend afternoons, when she knew she would run into them. "I tried meeting them for lunch a few times," she recalled, "but those meetings didn't work out because I was always distracted by my baby and felt out of place in my jeans. They would all chuck him under the chin and then leave me to deal with him while they discussed the latest office politics. Don't get me wrong — these women thought my baby was great — but these visits just didn't fit into the rhythm of the office day.

"Now I try to go down to the club at least one night a week while my husband takes over parenting chores. I get physical exercise, mental relief, and some fun with my old friends. When we're all rolling around on the floor in our sweats, our lives don't seem so different anymore."

Sometimes, despite your best efforts, lack of support can come from unexpected areas. One feminist at-home mother left her volunteer counseling job at a family planning clinic after fellow counselors started making unkind cracks about her third pregnancy. "What is it with you?" one of them asked her. "Don't you practice what you preach?" Although she was shocked to be challenged in such a way by a feminist colleague, the mother answered, "Of course I do. Three is how many I want."

While other people in the organization, including the female director, did support her decision to have more children, the atmosphere eventually became so uncomfortable that the mother left the clinic. She still considers herself an ardent feminist but is getting involved in local health and school board issues and staying away from the formal women's movement until, as she said, "feminism catches up with women."

Another woman found that her female coworkers gave her a hard time when she told them she planned to stay home. She told us, "I worked mostly with women, most of them bright, accomplished, capable, and successful. They were appalled at my decision to stay home with my child. I was told that I was betraying the women who had fought so hard for the rights and freedoms I took for granted, and that I was the kind of worker who made it hard for other women who planned to return to work after their maternity leaves. It made me very sad to discover that people were critical of one another at a time when they should stand united and become one another's help and support."

Others reported tremendous support, including offers of free baby-sitting and promises to send free-lance work the at-home mother's way. The important thing to remember is that whether you get support or condemnation, your colleagues' reactions have very little to do with you personally. These reactions are a reflection of their own feelings about themselves and their own struggles to balance work and family.

No matter how hard you try, there will be some drifting apart. The good news is that while old friends may grow distant, parenthood affords a wonderful opportunity to forge new relationships. A thirty-eight-year-old marketing manager, at home for two years with her twin daughters, said that "since being at home, I have made and developed more true friendships with other women than I ever had before." These new relationships with other mothers are often characterized by a closer, more intimate bond than that with office colleagues, with whom there may be an undercurrent of competition and distrust fostered by the corporate culture.

Another mother of twins said that she has found her greatest support (after her husband) in her local La Leche League group and has formed solid new friendships there. Secure in her new relationships, she simply "let go of old ones that were not supportive or were critical of my new life-style."

Even beyond the inevitable changes in life-style that parenthood brings, some people are forced by circumstances to develop a whole new set of friends, as in the case of one couple who relocated while the woman was pregnant. The woman, who didn't know anybody and didn't have the easy access to new relationships an office environment affords, suffered terribly from isolation. Still, she and her husband went on to have a second child. Today she swears that if she could do it all over again, she "wouldn't work while the kids were young, but I would *make absolutely sure* that I had a well-established social network."

For more on establishing networks, both private and public, see Chapters 9 and 10.

The "Mommy Wars"

At-home mothers should feel a sense of empathy with employed mothers, but this is often not the case. Unfortunately, relationships between at-home mothers and mothers who work outside the home are sometimes characterized by outright hostility. This hostility, which need not be inevitable, is detrimental to all mothers.

The so-called mommy wars are typified by the experience of one lawyer, who spent a long time making her decision to stay home and discussed it fully with her colleagues at work. She felt deeply hurt and betrayed to find that her most vocal critics were other professional women who were defensive about working long hours and missing their own children. Nonetheless, this woman made the decision to be a full-time parent and tried to put the hurt behind her.

Later, after her oldest child entered school, her sense of betrayal turned to resentment, as the unequal burden of fund-raising, trip supervision, and after-hours chauffeuring that she and the other full-time parents took on began to take its toll. Today, six years after

127

becoming a full-time mother, this woman cannot number one of her childless or working mother colleagues as a close friend.

Compare this mother's experience with that of a dedicated working mother who said that when she drops her son off at the bus stop on her way to work and sees a full-time mother in a tennis dress, she wants "to shoot her." This woman works a sixty-hour week and gets up an hour early so that she can have a leisurely breakfast with her son and daughter. She would love to be more involved with her local PTA or with other mothers in a play group, but she points out that most of the meetings and activities are scheduled for weekday mornings, when it is impossible for her to attend. Although she tried participating in these types of events on a part-time or as-able basis, she got tired of the other women's snide comments suggesting that she was an inadequate parent because she loved both her job and her children.

The irony of this situation is that both employed and at-home mothers believe they are doing what is best for themselves and their children. And, as our survey shows, they are very likely to switch roles. In fact, it's a false premise that women can only be placed on one side or the other of this issue. The *Wall Street Journal* reported the results of a study showing that most mothers go through both of these stages — working and staying home with their children — at different times in their lives. A sociologist who researched the work patterns of more than 2,000 young mothers found that "the great majority of women follow paths substantially more diverse than steady career or steady stay-at-home." She discovered that women tend to move back and forth from one role to another several times throughout their working and parenting careers as their children grow older or as new babies come along.[2]

Why should intolerance accompany our different choices, when our common experience should bring us together? The underlying reasons for these mommy wars — hostility, fear, and resentment — have been examined in numerous articles. While much of the media's coverage of "mommy vs. mommy" (as *Newsweek* called it in a feature story) has been exaggerated, there is some truth to their accounts of this conflict. Working mothers may be anxious about leaving their kids and feel guilty that they look forward to being at work. They naturally resent at-home mothers who imply that they don't love their children enough.

Conversely, at-home mothers may be anxious about their sense of identity and feel guilty about "wasting" their education. They naturally resent working mothers who imply that they aren't working or impose on them to chauffeur kids, watch out for the repairman, or put together a costume for a play. As Kate White, former editor of *Child* magazine, says, "In the '60s, the working mother was on the defensive. Then the non-working mother was on the defensive. Now everybody's defensive."[3]

Ambivalence about the choices they have made also can create hostility between women. Cynthia Copeland Lewis points out in her book *Mother's First Year,* "The more doubts a woman has over her own selection of an occupation, the more she perceives the other side as a threat and overcompensates for her inner conflict with public condemnation of those who are different."[4]

On both sides of this issue resentment stems not from a true war between women, but from the outmoded, inflexible model of work and family life that is present in our society as a whole. Women tend to see these problems as personal when in fact they are social. Society says that women at home don't work, that work is the only thing that validates a person, but that children are terribly important. Then it criticizes women who work outside the home for neglecting their children. If individual women internalize these illogical critiques, they will inevitably turn on each other, instead of directing their anger at a system that does not provide options for parents to balance their lives however they wish.

Much of this tension also comes from a lack of understanding of each other's lives. A twenty-eight-year-old mother reported that her relationship with her sisters-in-law has deteriorated since she chose to stay home. They criticized her for giving up her professional career and even told her that their children were better off in day care than her son was at home with her, since she is not a trained child-care worker. She told us, "I've done what my sisters-in-law are doing now (working full-time), but they haven't done what I'm doing. I was a working mom for a year, and I can understand the stress they're under, but they have no idea what I do. They just can't fathom it."

The truth is that at-home and working mothers have a lot in common. They are all dealing with the same challenges of parenting — sleepless nights, toilet training, battles with two-year-olds and adolescents, and raising their children the best way they can — but have come up with different solutions. The focus for parents, and for society in general, should be on making more options available and expanding the range of solutions to fit individual situations, instead of saying, "Thus and so is the only right solution, and I took it and you didn't." (For more on expanding the range of work/family solutions, see Chapter 9.)

In your personal life and interpersonal relationships, what can you do to lessen the tension and build a common ground? Donna Malone is an at-home mother who works part-time in an executive marketing research position and so has a foot in both camps. She has encountered stereotyped thinking from both sides. She said, "I have seen more prejudice among at-home mothers against working moms than the other way around. When I worked full-time and was dressed in a suit when I took my child to McDonald's after work, I felt that all the at-home moms were looking at me and saying, 'Isn't she a terrible mother?' "

On the other hand, Donna reported that many of the people she works with don't understand her decision to stay home and don't realize that she is under as much pressure as they are. She remembers calling the office one day and being asked by the receptionist, "How does it feel to live a life of leisure?" when she had been up until 2 A.M. that morning trying to complete a work project after spending the day with her daughters.

The best solution to this mutual resentment is to work at creating authentic relationships between at-home and working mothers. If you want participation from employed mothers, make an effort to keep community events accessible. Consider scheduling some of these events on weekends or in the evening. An accessible scheduling policy also will bring in more fathers, which promotes total family involvement.

Don't affirm yourself by putting someone else down. Recognize that both you and the other mother are reacting to society's unrealistic, idealized versions of motherhood and apply *Ground rule number 4: Consider yourself a feminist.* The other mothers are your sisters. Don't be guilty of perpetuating working mother myths, and avoid making statements that would hurt another mother. How can you rise up while putting your sister down?

Mary Clauss, a marketing manager at home with an eighteen-month-old son and a new baby, has a positive attitude toward mothers' differences: "I respect working mothers. It's hard for women to find their niche and know what they want to do. I try not to assume what I'm doing is right for all women, because it isn't."

In contrast, one adamantly at-home mother told us frankly, "You want the truth? I think if you're working because you have to earn money, it's fine. If you're working because of your ego, then you're cheating your child and it's selfish. I think dumping your kid in day care for twelve hours a day is wrong." Such a comment only escalates conflict and emphasizes differences.

It is truly egotistical to assume that you know what is right for everyone. Sometimes differences can be a source of strength between women. For example, Sandy, an at-home mother of two preschoolers, baby-sat for another neighbor's child on an emergency basis when her regular baby-sitter fell through. Sandy was initially worried about this arrangement because she felt the other mother, who worked forty hours a week, would never repay the favor. As it turned out, Sandy was wrong. Shortly afterward, her neighbor planned a special weekend outing with her own child to the zoo and park, and she offered to take Sandy's children along. Any at-home mother will tell you that a Saturday or Sunday alone with her husband is manna from heaven!

We know of another working mother, an emergency room nurse, who felt very guilty about always asking her at-home neighbor to sign for packages or let repair people in. She knew it was an imposition and was troubled by the fact that she couldn't reciprocate — until the day her neighbor needed to find a new pediatrician. Through her contacts at the hospital, the nurse was able to advise her neighbor on a topic of extreme importance to both of

131

them — children's health care. Although they lead very different lives, these women are able and willing to help make each other's lives a little easier.

These mothers found a way to make positive use of their differences instead of letting the differences divide them. It can be done. In the next chapter, we show you how building these mutually productive relationships, called networking, can make your life as an at-home mother easier and more satisfying.

8

Private Networking: Support Groups

It is comforting to know there are many women who are going through the same things that I am experiencing and are finding ways to cope.
— Rozanne Silverwood, *former health center administrator and at-home mother*[1]

Along with a supportive husband, having a support group of like-minded women is essential if you want to enjoy your life as an at-home mother. Even if you don't get much respect from the outside world, you can survive those sleepless nights of early motherhood and thrive in your new career if you find a group of friends who understand and value the work you do.

Professional women today know all about the benefits of networking for their careers. Women at home are no different. The more you can join with other full-time mothers, the easier and more fun your mothering job will be. After all, these are your new colleagues and coworkers.

To get started, consider joining a play group or mothers' organization, since it can be hard to find colleagues to talk to once you're at home. You may think that you can find all the new friends you need by following women with strollers down the street or casually bumping into them at the neighborhood park. Unfortunately, many neighborhoods don't have any other mothers who are currently at home. Even if you do find some other mothers nearby, just because you're all at home doesn't mean you have a lot in common besides children. By joining a support group, you're more likely to find other women who share your interests and values.

Joining a mothers' organization has many other advantages. Formal support groups can offer meetings and speakers that keep your mind from getting rusty, an opportunity to keep your work skills sharp through volunteering for the group, a chance to become a leader in the organization and get involved in your community, and a way to make a visible contribution to something outside of your family. Sherri McCarthy is very involved with helping to plan and run her local Mothers' Center. She told us, "This work with the group has allowed me to use my talents and gain positive feedback for my efforts. I am still doing work and producing results that I am proud of. This has been important in bolstering my self-image as an at-home mom."

This chapter offers step-by-step advice on how you can go about satisfying your need for adult company and friendship. We start on the local level and look at ways to find or start a play group or baby-sitting co-op. Then we give you an up-to-date resource list of the major national and regional support groups for at-home mothers, including interviews with several of their founders.

Everything You Need to Know About Play Groups

Being a mother can be a lonely business. While children can be endearing companions, their conversational abilities leave something to be desired. At-home mothers who were used to lots of adult interaction in the office may feel especially isolated. It's not as easy as it used to be to walk out the front door of your house or apartment and find ready-made female friends and playmates for your children.

Today mothers at home need to be more creative and assertive in finding each other. Where can you go for on-the-job feedback and support in your career as an at-home mother? Play groups are one answer. Thousands of play groups, which offer social activities and supervised play for a small group of women and their children, have sprung up around the country during the past few years.

Where can you find a play group? Keep an eye out for mothers' groups already organized in your own community and consult the list of national mothers' groups later in this chapter. Local newspapers, libraries, church and temple groups, YWCAs, and supermarket bulletin boards often list groups that are looking for new members.

Some groups prefer to limit their members to friends and friends of friends, to make sure they share traits and child-raising philosophies. We know of one mother, Marilyn, who was very disappointed in the first play group she joined. She was a new mother who noticed a play group meeting weekly at her local park and thought it would be a good way to make friends and share experiences. As it turned out, it was not a good match. The other women were all mothers of two or three children, and they kept giving her unwanted advice and lectures. "Instead of being my peers, they were more like my mother!" Marilyn exclaimed. She decided it was best to leave the group when the other mothers criticized her for continuing to breast-feed her baby when they felt she should start weaning him.

It can save a lot of time and grief later on if you talk with potential play group members before you join and make sure you agree on the basic ground rules. You can continue to use the skills you developed in the workplace in organizing your play group, planning occasional meetings, and establishing rapport with your new colleagues. Typical play group rules cover deciding how often and where to meet, whether to serve food and drinks at each meeting, coming up with a policy on whether sick children may come to the meetings, and choosing who will be in charge of planning group events.

Women with varied backgrounds can make fine group members. You don't necessarily want a group that agrees on everything. However, problems may arise between women who have radically different ideas on child raising — for instance, those who see no harm in spanking and those who consider it grounds for calling the child abuse hot line. If conflicts emerge despite all your precautions, it's probably best to seek a new group. There's no point in having a miserable time each week when a congenial group could be down the block.

If you can't find an existing group, consider starting your own. Recruit play group members by keeping an eye out for women with young children in your area. Good places to spot them are at the YMCA, Lamaze classes, park district classes, neighborhood associations, and local women's groups or by placing a small classified ad in your newspaper. You may have to strike up a conversation with a total stranger on the street or in a store. Don't be discouraged if the first few people you approach aren't interested, and don't expect instant friendship if they are interested. Be prepared to spend time developing your play group relationships.

Plan to meet at one of the group members' houses to begin with to work out a schedule. Meeting once a week for a couple of hours (usually in the morning, to avoid nap times) often works best. It's a good idea to limit the group to between four and seven women, since a group with more than ten young children can be noisy and chaotic when they're all in full cry in a small house. Try to find women with children of similar ages. It also makes sense to have one member in charge of phoning all the members to let them know about the next week's meeting place and any changes in plans.

In good weather, a visit to a park or a field trip can be an ideal way to keep a group of active children happy. If you have younger children in your group, try to find a local "tot lot" — a park with safe, small-scale play equipment made for babies and toddlers. Remember that parks with grass or wood chips are much safer than those with a concrete surface. Look for plenty of shade trees for those humid summer days and park benches for the moms. Having a bathroom right there also is a must for children who are in the midst of toilet training (not to mention expectant mothers).

One group we know meets at a different park every week. Variety is fun for the children, and it gives you a chance to try out parks you might not have known about. Or you might enjoy planning field trips to a children's museum, a nearby zoo, an amusement park, a swimming pool or lake (with lifeguards), or a pizza or ice cream parlor. A short train ride (the destination doesn't matter) also can be fun.

In bad weather, you can take turns hosting the group at each other's homes. If your group gets too large, you might ask a nearby community college or neighborhood community center if it has any spare rooms. Many schools and civic centers offer meeting rooms at no charge, which can beat having ten kids stampede across your living room on a rainy day. It's a good idea to have snacks and juice for the children. This can cut down on grumpiness and serve as a quiet time for all.

Play groups can do more than provide an opportunity for free play. While many groups have a loose, relaxed atmosphere, others have more structured game times, with a weekly art project, science lesson, or fitness program. This usually works best with children older than three, since younger children may not have a sufficient attention span or motor skills. You can take turns with the other mothers in planning and leading these learning activities. Most libraries have resource books that have great ideas for creative games for parents and kids.

We suggest these resources to get started:

About.com's "Parenting: Babies & Toddlers" section has several articles
    on starting a playgroup
Newhomemaker.com's article "Start a Playgroup, Begin an Adventure"
The Playgroup Handbook by Laura Peabody Broad and Nancy Towner
    Butterworth (St. Martin's, 1991)

Play groups can be invaluable sources of moral support and practical assistance when mothers give birth or have to cope with a child's or parent's illness or other emergency. In these situations, it's great to have friends to provide you with hot meals, help look after your children, and give you some sympathy. This is especially important for women who may live far away from their families and need a local support structure to help them through difficult times.

Remember that play groups aren't just for the children. You may find that you are even more eager to come to the group each week than your children are. Having a time set aside for play group every week can give you something to look forward to, a reason to get out of the house, and the chance to enjoy the company of other women while comparing notes on child raising. For most play group members, the group has become a vital part of their personal support network.

Baby-Sitting Co-ops

Play groups have many benefits, but they do not offer you the chance to have time for yourself away from your children. Teenage baby-sitters can be impossible to find during the school day, and many women find it hard to justify the expense of hiring a sitter, especially when so many families are taking an economic hit so that one spouse can be at home. At-home mothers who are not bringing home a salary often have a very hard time justifying spending money on themselves. This situation can be extremely detrimental to the full-time mother, who is often in dire need of personal time to sleep, read, exercise, attend a meeting or show, and reestablish contact with adult reality.

A baby-sitting co-op is an organized network of parents who trade their baby-sitting services for free child care for their own children. Some play group members also develop a co-op. A cardinal rule for co-ops is to keep track of the number of hours each mother spends baby-sitting and make sure she receives one hour of baby-sitting for each hour she donates as a sitter. It is important to be serious about keeping the account book current, since this acknowledges the value of the time a mother spends taking care of children and also ensures that no one will feel shortchanged.

To get started, you'll need to find several other mothers or couples who live nearby and are interested in becoming a part of the co-op. Some co-ops have as few as five couples, but we have heard of others with as many as forty. Having more than a dozen families can ensure that you can always find a baby-sitter when you need one, but you don't want the co-op to get so large that it's hard to get to know most of the members. Plan a general meeting where you can get acquainted and set up an organizational plan. Then plan to meet every quarter to keep up-to-date with new members and to discuss any co-op business.

138

Most co-ops use index cards or printed business cards as the medium of exchange, although you could use photocopied coupons or play money. New members generally receive a stack of cards entitling them to free baby-sitting. One card represents one-half hour of baby-sitting time. If you go out to a movie for three hours, you would pay six cards to the parent taking care of your child. Many co-ops charge one card per hour for each additional child in the family.

To find a sitter, a member simply goes through the co-op list and calls other parents until she finds someone who says yes. She then drops her child off at the other parent's house at the agreed-upon time. If you start running out of cards, it's a good idea to put in some time baby-sitting another co-op family's children so that you receive more cards.

Keeping a complicated co-op working smoothly is a lot like running a small business. Each co-op needs to appoint a leader or manager who is given the opportunity to apply her organizational, computing, and interpersonal skills. The leader's job is to maintain and update the list of co-op care givers and their children, tabulate the number of hours of baby-sitting each couple provides and receives each month, and iron out any differences among co-op members.

Leadership rotates among co-op members every three months or so, depending on the co-op's size. Many groups issue a monthly update listing information such as which days or nights a couple is usually available for baby-sitting and details about the children's diets, favorite toys, and bedtime routines. Denise Lang offers a helpful example of a child information sheet in her book *The Phantom Spouse* (see box on page 140). She notes:

Each parent should fill out a form for each of her children participating in the co-op process. . . . Each participating mother or father should receive a stapled packet that includes an information sheet on each child as well as a cover sheet listing all the members, with addresses and telephone numbers. This way, when she is asked to babysit Johnny, she can look up Johnny's information, note that he is allergic to apple juice, and his favorite show is Mr. Rogers. This will make babysitting Johnny a safer and more pleasant experience all the way around.²

Other co-ops are very informal and can consist of just two mothers who take turns caring for each other's children. For example, two friends developed a system that worked well for them. Sheila took care of Judy's children all day on Mondays, and Judy returned the favor on Fridays. As a result, each mother had an entire day to herself to spend as she pleased — true bliss for a harried

---

Babysitting Co-op Child Information Sheet

Child's name:	Date of birth:
Address:	Phone:
Mother's name:	Business phone:
Father's name:	Business phone:
Pediatrician's name:	Phone:

In case of emergency: (someone other than working parent)
Phone:
Medical authorization:
Child's allergies:

(a) Medicine:
(b) Food:
(c) Other:
Child's special likes:
Child's special dislikes:
Child's favorite TV shows:
Any additional comments helpful in caring for your child:

From *The Phantom Spouse* by Denis V. Lang. Reprinted by permission from Betterway Publications, Inc.

---

mother. Judy was an active member of a local mothers' group, and she used her day off to catch up on her board work. This enabled her to have weekends and evenings free to be with her family, instead of frantically trying to get her work done when her husband was home and feeling guilty about not spending any time with him. Sheila used her Fridays as well-earned personal days. She would have lunch with an office friend, go shopping, do aerobics, catch a matinee, read a novel, or take a long nap. This relaxing time to herself kept her from getting grouchy with the kids and having regrets about her decision to stay home with them.

An arrangement with a friend can be easy to make, but it is important that you set up ground rules before you begin. Many mothers prefer to start with one morning a week and then expand to two mornings (or to full days) once they and their children are more comfortable with this arrangement. Before you begin, sit down and talk over all the details you can think of, so no unpleasant surprises will come up. Ask the other mother: When are your children's nap times? What do they prefer to eat for snacks or lunch? Are there any food allergies or other health matters I should know about? What are their favorite games and toys? What rules of discipline do you want me to enforce?

There will be days when one or more of the children are sick or you have other plans, so try to set up alternative days beforehand as a backup. We suggest that you stay by a phone the first couple of times you leave your child with the other mother in case she has any questions for you. If your child is still in the middle of separation anxiety and screams when you leave her with a sitter, try to ease her into this arrangement slowly. Come and stay at your friend's house with her for an hour or two for the first couple of weeks until she is more comfortable with her surroundings. In addition, make sure you both have well-stocked first aid kits and have signed permission from the other mother to authorize emergency health care if needed. With preschoolers, accidents are bound to happen, and you want to be as prepared as possible.

At its best, this baby-sitting arrangement can be a wonderful way for your children to make a close friend or two, as well as to give you a well-deserved break.

Mothers' Support Groups

One of the easiest ways to network with other women who have chosen motherhood as a career is to join one of the mothers' support organizations. These groups can be divided into three categories (although some of them overlap): primarily support groups, parent education groups, and family service organizations. In the remainder of this chapter, we provide information about groups in each category, featuring several organizations that are specifically for at-home mothers. Our resource list also includes groups that are open to all parents but have a large proportion of at-home mothers in their membership. Each listing includes detailed information about the group's benefits and characteristics to help you determine which one might be right for you.[3]

Mothers & More (formerly known as FEMALE)

Mothers & More is a support and advocacy network for sequencing women—mothers who have altered their career paths in order to care for their children at home. It differs from other mothers' organizations by addressing women's personal needs and interests during their active parenting years, and by advocating for public and employment policies that accommodate sequencing (moving in and out of the paid workforce as family needs and realities dictate).

This national nonprofit association began in 1987 after Joanne Brundage, a postal worker, left her job because she was unable to find adequate child care for her children. Faced with the loss of self-esteem, identity and financial security her job had given her, Brundage found herself depressed and unsure about her new role. She placed an ad in her local paper looking for other mothers who were having trouble making the transition from an outside career to at-home mothering. Four women answered the ad and helped start the support group. Today Mothers & More has over 8,000 members, 180 local chapters across the United States, and one chapter in the United Kingdom. Mothers & More's diverse membership includes women who are home with their children full-time, work from home, work part-time, freelance, or cut back on their work hours in order to raise their families.

This organization was originally known as FEMALE (an acronym for "Formerly Employed Mothers At Loose Ends"). The name was changed to "Formerly Employed Mothers at the Leading Edge" in 1991 to describe the group's commitment to advocacy. In June 2000, a new name was announced. "Mothers & More" was chosen because "mothers want *more*: more time with their children, more work options that allow them to spend more time parenting, more respect for their choice to focus on family above career," explained Pam Hainlin, Mothers & More president. Mothers & More provides its members:

- local chapter affiliation—evening meetings, guest speakers
- "Moms' Night Out" activities, book discussions, playgroups, family outings and more
- *The FORUM*—a bimonthly publication focusing on work and family issues, survival techniques, book reviews, author interviews, and other topics for sequencing mothers
- online services—an interactive website (www.mothersandmore.org) offering e-mail loops, online chats, message boards, events calendar, news and monthly discussion topics
- leadership opportunities—the chance to keep work skills current or acquire new ones by volunteering for the organization

Contact: Mothers & More, P.O. Box 31, Elmhurst, IL 60126; 800-223-9399 or (630) 941-3553. E-mail: Nationaloffice@mothersandmore.org. Website: www.mothersandmore.org. Annual membership is $45.

Interview with Joanne Brundage, Mothers & More Founder

Why did you decide to start this group?
    This organization began because I quit full-time work after my second child was born and found myself alone and miserable. I put myself in all the places I could think of to meet other at-home mothers, but I couldn't find one who understood or shared the problems I was facing after working for so many years.

What's the organization's history?
    Mothers & More grew from five members initially to over eight thousand

today. We started out thinking that we were exceptions in having trouble adjusting to life at home, but, obviously, we no longer feel that way! When we got our group mentioned in *Ms.*, *Parents*, and other national magazines, women really responded to our name then, which was "Formerly Employed Mothers At Loose Ends." That's part of the reason we grew so rapidly. But our current name is more descriptive of the group today, as it seeks to offer women the personal support they need and to influence society to change its work and family priorities. And, although our organization serves mothers making family and work choices other than full-time employment, Mothers & More respects and supports all mothers' choices involving work and family.

What were the hardest things about starting and running this group?

It was difficult to go public with my advertisement without knowing whether there was one other person on this earth who felt the same way. The most difficult thing to do once we got started was to avoid the familiar habit of talking about our children and child-rearing issues. My goal in starting the group was for us to be able to relate to each other as adults with interests in subjects other than children, and for that to be OK.

What does Mothers & More offer its members?

We offer women what they've told us for over a decade that they want and need most--friends and a sense of community with women in the same situation. Thanks to our newly expanded website, our members can meet other moms both in their communities and across the country via our online chats, book discussions and the like. We also provide women a safe place to reestablish their self worth and redefine their identity. We're able to do that both through friendship and through leadership opportunities.

At the same time, we are a national network that provides mothers the tools and the voice to make employers, government and society more accountable to the needs of women and their families. We recognized early on that the issues we shared were not solely personal ones, but were brought on by society's lack of true commitment to women and children.

The not-so-secret of Mothers & More's success is that our members have offered our organization their formidable skills, talents and dedication in return. Our member volunteers have made the organization what it is today!

La Leche League International

La Leche League International (LLLI) was one of the first national support groups for mothers. Founded by seven Chicago-area women in 1956, this nonprofit organization offers practical information, education and encouragement to all mothers who want to breastfeed their babies. When the League started, less than one-quarter of new American mothers tried nursing their babies for even a short period of time. Today, largely because of the organization's efforts, sixty percent of American mothers breastfeed their babies. The League celebrated its 40th anniversary in 1996, and has grown to 27,000 members and 3,000 LLLI support groups in 56 countries.

While breastfeeding is its primary focus, LLLI also offers mothers a chance to find support, develop friendships, and learn more about parenting through local meetings and a bimonthly magazine. Mary White, one of the group's founders, has said, "Our purpose is and always has been to 'foster good mothering through breastfeeding,' and by so doing, to encourage good physical and emotional growth for the child and the development of closer and happier family relationships."

LLLI's members include both employed and at-home mothers. The League attracts a large number of mothers who decided to stay home because they wanted the freedom to breastfeed their babies on demand.

Mothers interested in using their leadership skills can find plenty of opportunities in this organization to lead a group. More than 8,000 volunteer leaders, who are experienced breastfeeding mothers, run local support groups and provide personal mother-to-mother help. The League assists its leaders through a comprehensive handbook and a bimonthly leaders' publication. LLLI offers these benefits of membership:

- informal, monthly group discussion meetings held in members' homes
- a bimonthly magazine, *New Beginnings*
- telephone assistance for mothers who have nursing questions or problems

- a 10 percent discount on purchases of breastfeeding products and LLLI publications, including the popular handbook *The Womanly Art of Breastfeeding*
- annual regional and international conferences
- numerous resources offered through www.lalecheleague.org, including answers to breastfeeding questions, links to LLLI leaders in all 50 US states and 27 countries, and web-based chats on Moms Online and Parent Soup

Contact: La Leche League International, P.O. Box 4079, Schaumburg, IL 60168-4079; 1-800-La Leche or (847) 519-7730. E-mail: LLLHQ@llli.org. Website: www.llli.org. Annual membership is $30.

MOMS Club

The MOMS Club is a national network of support groups specifically for at-home mothers. This rapidly-growing nonprofit organization currently has 50,000 members in more than 1,000 local chapters across the country. The first group, originally known as the "Moms Offering Moms Support" Club, was started in California in 1983. Three years later, the MOMS Club became a national organization.

The club welcomes mothers with children of all ages. The organization's goals are "to provide a support group for mothers who choose to stay at home to raise their children; to provide a forum for topics of interest to mothers; to help children in the community; and to perform at least one service project yearly helping needy children."

All meetings and most activities are held during the day, when mothers at home need support the most. Children are welcome to attend every club event. Local chapters offer a wide range of activities, including:

- monthly meetings with speakers and discussions
- playgroups and babysitting co-ops
- a monthly MOMS Night Out
- special activity groups related to members' interests, such as exercise groups, arts and crafts and book clubs

146

- play days at the park, outings, family get-togethers, and community service projects
- the national website, www.momsclub.org, provides lists and contact numbers for its chapters and a members-only national newsletter

Each local chapter is registered with the national MOMS Club but operates independently. Chapters have the freedom to elect their own officers, set dues, and choose their own speakers and programming. The national office provides volunteer coordinators and a detailed manual to help women who want to start their own local MOMS club, and organizes regional activities in areas where there are several clubs.

Contact: MOMS Club, 25371 Rye Canyon, Valencia, CA 91355. Use e-mail to reach MOMS, or enclose $2 if you're requesting information by mail. E-mail: momsclub@aol.com. Website: www.momsclub.org. Each chapter sets its own dues, usually between $15 to $25 a year.

Interview with Mary James, Founder of the MOMS Club

Why did you decide to start this group?
    When I decided to stay home, I was literally the only mother I personally knew at home. All my friends were working and simply could not relate to my new life. I hadn't even been around babies before my first daughter was born, and I had no role models to look up to. When I turned on the TV, even the daytime shows for women like 'Hour Magazine,' all I heard was 'How to choose good daycare,' 'How to interview for a job,' 'Dressing for success.'
    All the pieces were how to succeed on the job--nothing about how to survive staying home. That's why I started the MOMS Club: to fill that very empty niche of supporting at-home mothers, and accepting and nurturing their decision to stay home for their families.
    I started the first MOMS Club in California in 1983, but from the immediate response I got, I knew that other mothers across the country must be feeling the same sense of loneliness and neglect that I had felt. As members spread the work of what we had started, their friends in other communities asked to start local MOMS Clubs of their own.

What is your group's philosophy?

The MOMS Club's positive attitude sets us apart. Many mothers' groups presume that mothers at home need either teaching or tender care, such as the local support groups started by hospitals' mental health outreach programs. We believe that mothers at home are neither stupid nor insane and should be treated as adults who have made an honored sacrifice to help their families and society.

MOPS (Mothers of Preschoolers) International

This international support group has a Christian focus. MOPS International describes itself as "a nonprofit Christian outreach ministry, dedicated to nurturing mothers of preschoolers (infants to six years old) . . . and providing resources directly to moms." Founded in 1973, MOPS currently has 2,500 chapters in the United States, Canada, and ten other countries.

MOPS is dedicated to the message that "mothering matters," and that moms of young children need encouragement during these critical and formative years. Chartered groups meet in churches of various denominations. Each MOPS program helps mothers find friendship and acceptance, provides opportunities for women to develop and practice leadership skills by volunteering in the group, and promotes spiritual growth in its members. This organization offers:

- regular group meetings which address current issues in child rearing, womanhood, the home and relationships, based on biblical principles
- small discussion groups led by mothers
- creative activities and crafts at each meeting
- special MOPS groups designed for teens, urban mothers, evening and work place groups
- childcare and planned activities provided for young children during MOPS meetings
- *MomSense Magazine*, a bimonthly publication that offers encouraging tips and ideas
- MOMSense Radio, a two-minute daily feature that airs on 500 U.S. radio stations

148

- leadership training, regional conferences and national conventions
- www.mops.org offers information on joining and starting a local MOPS group, MOPS events, and an online store

Contact: MOPS International, P.O. Box 102200, Denver, CO 80250-2200; 800-929-1287 or (303) 733-5353. E-mail: info@mops.org. Website: www.mops.org. Annual membership is $15.

Mothers at Home

Mothers at Home was started by three Northern Virginia women in 1984 to support mothers who choose (or would like to choose) to stay home with their children. Instead of offering face-to-face support groups, this nonprofit organization helps women through its award-winning *Welcome Home* publication, a monthly magazine with 24,000 subscribers.

The organization's mission is to "affirm the choice to be home throughout the many stages of motherhood; provide mother-to-mother support, education and networking; correct society's misconceptions and refute stereotypes about parents and children; serve as advocates for parents and children; and enable mothers to preserve and improve the opportunity for all women to choose home."

Mothers at Home describes its magazine this way: "*Welcome Home* is for the smart woman who has actively chosen to devote her time and talents to nurturing her family." *Welcome Home* serves as a forum for at-home mothers across the country to share their feelings and insights on mothering.

This organization is also active in representing at-home mothers to the government and the media. By speaking to mothers' groups, giving media interviews, and testifying before Congress on issues important to women and families, Mothers at Home furthers the interests of women at home caring for their children.

Contact: Mothers at Home, 9493-C Silver King Ct, Fairfax, VA 22031;

800-783-4666 or (703) 352-1072. E-mail: mah@mah.org. Website: www.mah.org. *Welcome Home's* annual subscription rate is $18.

Interview with Heidi L. Brennan, former Co-Director of Mothers at Home

How did Mothers at Home become a successful national organization?
Mothers at Home got a lot of media attention fast, as soon as the first article appeared in the *Washington Post*. In three months, we went from planning to have two hundred friends as subscribers to thirty-five hundred subscribers. The group grew from an idea to fifteen thousand subscribers in seven years without a big public relations or marketing effort.

We now have a large office, with enough space for mothers to come in and work for our expanded organization, and a large playroom for our children. What is remarkable about our organization's success is that we capitalized the whole operation from its own subscription revenue. Mothers at Home was started from a few hundred dollars put up by the founders. None of us was financially experienced to begin with. The learning we all have done is beyond belief. It beats anything I learned in graduate school.

What does your organization offer at-home mothers, and what do you consider its greatest accomplishments?
Welcome Home shows mothers at home that their feelings and concerns are shared, and we give our members a sense of empowerment. Our organization wants to shift other people's thinking of mothers at home. We want others to understand the importance of our work.

Isolation and economics are constant problems for mothers at home, and we offer help through our magazine. I'm proud that we continuously produce a supportive publication that is substantial in size and provides an opportunity for women to speak. All of our articles come from members. We don't turn *Welcome Home* over to professionals: mothers are the experts.

We also speak out on behalf of mothers to other groups and to the government. We've been able to do that partly because of our access to Washington, D.C. One of the biggest surprises we encountered was how hard it is to work with the major media. Reporters love it when you talk about the down side of motherhood; they always magnify it in their articles. So we don't talk about that. We try to stress that motherhood is complex, that it's a joy and a great choice for women to make.

150

What are Mothers at Home's goals for the future?
We plan to continue to educate public policy and media people about mothers at home. We want to work with other mothers' groups on this too, as part of a grass roots effort. Our other goal is to develop special publications on special topics. Mothers at Home has published a few books: *What's a Smart Woman Like You Doing at Home?*, *Discovering Motherhood*, which is about making the transition to motherhood at home, and *Motherhood: Journey into Love*.

Hearts at Home

Founded in 1994 by Jill Savage, Hearts at Home began as a small Christian organization for mothers at home in Central Illinois. A former teacher, Savage had always enjoyed attending annual teachers' conferences. She began to wonder if anyone offered conferences for women who had decided to stay home to nurture their families.

Savage decided she would like to bring the latest information on parenting to women in a conference setting. She wanted to give women the opportunity to meet some of their favorite authors, receive some education, and get a much-needed break from responsibilities at home. When the group decided to put on a regional conference, they were surprised and delighted when 1,100 women from ten different states attended their first conference. Hearts at Home now has 30,000 women who want to learn about upcoming conferences on their mailing list.

The organization's mission is to educate and encourage mothers at home and those who want to be. Hearts at Home believes that motherhood is a valid profession. It describes its regional conferences as "an opportunity for a weekend getaway packed full of new ideas for moms who consider mothering their career choice." The conferences feature well-known speakers and authors and offer a variety of practical workshops for mothers. Hearts at Home also produces:

- *Hearts at Home* monthly magazine, which features articles by conference keynote speakers and at-home moms

- a web page, www.hearts-at-home.org, with up-to-date information about Hearts at Home's conferences, a bulletin board, and e-mail newsletter
- a Mom's Referral Network that helps women connect with other moms' support groups in their area, and also serves as a clearinghouse for secular and Christian publications for at-home moms
- a monthly devotional designed to help mothers at home make prayer a part of their days
- audiotapes from past conferences available for sale

Contact: Hearts at Home, 900 W. College Avenue, Normal, IL 61761; (309) 888-6667. E-mail: hearts@dave-world.net. Website: www.hearts-at-home.org. Annual subscription to *Hearts at Home* magazine is $15. Annual subscription to their monthly devotional is $20. Conferences cost $50 to attend.

Home-Based Working Moms

This is a professional association and online community of parents who work at home or aspire to work at home. Lesley Spencer founded HBWM in 1995, shortly after the birth of her first child. After she quit her full-time job and started a home-based business, she saw that parents working at home need support, information, and networking opportunities.

Most HBWM members are like their founder—they create home-based careers in order to spend more time with their children. One member described this organization as "a national community of women using each other's services and offering suggestions while truly supporting each other's ventures."

Members are notified about new home-based and freelance work opportunities when companies contact HBWM looking for home-based workers. The association's website—www.hbwm.com— is dedicated to helping moms find work and avoid scams. Members' benefits include:

- a monthly newsletter features successful home-based working moms, home business information and marketing tips
- a weekly e-newsletter
- an e-mail discussion listserve where members can meet other HBWMs, get advice, and make new friends
- access to HBWM's panel of experts, who can answer questions on everything from accounting and legal issues to balancing a home business and children
- opportunities for members to promote their products and services

Contact: Home-Based Working Mothers, P.O. Box 500164, Austin, TX 78750; (512) 918-0670. E-mail: getinfo@hbwm.com. Website: www.hbwm.com. Annual membership is $44.

Mocha Moms

Mocha Moms is a support group for mothers of color who have chosen not to work full-time outside the home in order to devote more time to their families. Mocha Moms also serves as an advocate for at-home mothers of color and encourages the spirit of community activism within its membership. This organization welcomes people of all religions, races, educational backgrounds and income levels. Anyone who supports Mocha Moms' mission is welcome to join.

Mocha Moms began in 1997, when Jolene Ivey and Karla Chustz began publishing a newsletter for mothers of color. The organization still publishes this quarterly newsletter. The newsletter's purpose is to encourage mothers to feel good about their choice to stay home and to provide information to help them be the best and most important influence in their children's lives. Mocha Moms also supports women through their website. The website can be used as a resource for current members, prospective members, or anyone else interested in at-home parenting.

They have two local chapters in Maryland and one in Washington, D.C., and are accepting applications for new chapters. Dues are purposely kept low so there are no financial barriers to joining. The chapters offer:

- weekly playgroups
- a monthly moms-only potluck dinner
- community projects

Contact: Mocha Moms, 2800 Valley Way, Cheverly, MD 20785; 301-322-8190. E-mail: info@mochamoms.org. Website: www.mochamoms.org. Annual membership is $12.

National Association of At-Home Mothers

The National Association of At-Home Mothers is a professional organization that offers women support for the career choice of at-home parenting. Like Mothers at Home, this organization does not offer local chapters. The NAAHM primarily supports mothers through its glossy quarterly publication, *At-Home Mother* magazine. Jeanette Lisefski, the founder, described the group's purpose: "Our mission is simple: to support the at-home motherhood lifestyle. We are not an advocacy group, nor do we have a religious or political agenda. We simply offer practical information, inspiration, services, support and encouragement for mothers at home and those who would like to be."

Through their publications and website, the National Association of At-Home Mothers provides articles and resources that will help women enjoy their choice of at-home motherhood. Membership benefits include:

- *At-Home Mother* magazine, a full-color magazine that includes regular features on choosing home, making and saving money at home, self-esteem, celebrating motherhood, parenting, household management, home learning and personal growth
- *At-Home Mother News*, a newsletter that helps members stay up-to-date on the association's activities and benefits
- resources, links, and articles on their website: www.AtHomeMothers.com
- pamphlets offering practical information and solutions for at-home mothers' concerns
- AtHomeMothers.com Bookstore--member discounts

154

- the opportunity to apply for cash grants to start a home business

Contact: The National Association of At-Home Mothers, 406 East Buchanan Avenue, Fairfield, IA 52556. No phone number is listed. E-mail: information@AtHomeMothers.com. Website: www.AtHomeMothers.com. Annual membership is $18.

National Association of Mothers' Centers

The original Mothers' Center was started in Hicksville, New York, in 1974 by a group of women who were concerned that pregnancy and early child rearing are often times of struggle, confusion, and low self-confidence. They started a research project to identity mothers' unmet needs and in the process found that getting together to discuss information, ideas, and feelings about motherhood helped them cope with this stage of their lives. Today there are local Mothers' Centers in 18 states, and more are being started every year.

The NAMC is a nonprofit network of community groups where mothers can come together for support, education, and professional training. Each Mothers' Center is owned and run by the women themselves, and each center is different, depending on the needs of its local members and their own community.

The organization's overall goal is to support and validate the work of mothering. The NAMC states that they have a "unique commitment to all mothers--whether they are at home, working out of the home, adoptive, biological, or the myriad other choices they've made or circumstances they face."

The NAMC tends to attract women who are interested in actively helping other mothers and their families, as well as finding support for themselves. Members receive these benefits:

- regular meetings that feature supportive group discussions on child-rearing issues and problems; childcare is available during meetings

- informative workshops for mothers on the developmental needs of their children, their families, and themselves
- a comprehensive handbook on how to start a local Mothers' Center
- the chance to advocate for women and families and to improve life in their communities
- the NAMC's annual national conference provides networking opportunities, support and advice on establishing and sustaining local Mothers' Centers
- some Mothers' Centers also offer playgroups, "Mommy and Me" classes, and social activities

Contact: The National Association of Mothers' Centers (NAMC), 64 Division Avenue, Levittown, NY 11756; 800-645-3828 or (516) 520-2929. E-mail: info@motherscenter.org. Website: www.motherscenter.org. Fees vary.

National Parenting Association

The National Parenting Association was founded by author-activist Sylvia Ann Hewlett in 1993. Its goal is to give parents a greater voice in the public arena. This nonprofit, nonpartisan organization's primary goal is to build a parents' movement that unites mothers and fathers across the country. The NPA believes that "parenting is an important job that deserves our personal and public commitment. Parents can be the leading edge of social change."

To achieve their mission, the NPA listens to parents through surveys and their website; advocates private and public sector initiatives that give parents support; informs parents about issues; and helps them make their voices heard locally and in Washington, DC. The organization also seeks to promote positive images of parents and parenting through exhibits, publications and media campaigns. Through their Partners program, the NPA has joined forces with other groups to develop local programs that benefit parents and children.

The NPA also advocates for everyday practical support for mothers and fathers. The organization is in favor of flexible work options, tax breaks that help parents afford to take time off to care for their children and to pay for quality child care when they're at work, enriching after-school programs, and gun control laws. Through the organization's website, www.parentsunite.org, parents can find:

* ways to get involved with the NPA
* the opportunity to e-mail elected leaders about issues that matter to parents
* information on win-win solutions at work, at school and in communities, and good ideas that have helped other parents around the nation
* links to other organizations and resources for parents

Contact: National Parenting Association, 51 W. 74th Street, Suite 1B, New York, NY 10023; (212) 362-7575. E-mail: info@parentsunite.org. Website: www.parentsunite.org. No annual membership fee; donations are requested.

Attachment Parenting International (API)

API is a coalition of concerned parents, professionals, and grassroots organizations that advocate attachment parenting. Attachment parenting is "a style of parenting that develops an infant or child's need for trust, empathy, and affection in order to create a secure, peaceful, and enduring relationship." This style requires a consistent and nurturing caregiver, ideally a parent, especially during the critical first three years of life. API members believe that attachment parenting, in conjunction with support groups, can strengthen families and aid in the prevention of child abuse, behavioral disorders, and other serious social problems.

API was founded by Lysa Parker and Barbara Nicholson after they came across research on the importance of helping infants develop a secure attachment to a parent or primary caregiver. API's goals are to educate society about the psychological and emotional needs of babies and young children; to function as a resource center providing educational materials and support groups for parents, children, and the community; to empower women in all societies; and to promote the concepts of attachment parenting. Their ultimate goal is to encourage "peaceful parenting for a peaceful world." Membership benefits include:

- more than 50 parent support groups in the U.S. and Europe
- information on starting your own parent support group
- access to API's library of research and articles on childbirth, breastfeeding, parent education, positive discipline and attachment research
- a subscription to their quarterly newsletter, *API News*
- an e-mail newsletter and informative website

Contact: Attachment Parenting International,1508 Clairmont Place, Nashville, TN 37215; (615) 298-4334. E-mail: ATTParent@aol.com. Website: www.attachmentparenting.org. Annual membership is $30.

Regional and local mothers' groups

So many mothers' groups have been springing up throughout the United States that it's impossible to list all the regional groups. There are also hundreds of specialty parents' groups, such as support groups for mothers of twins, parents of only children, parents of children with special needs, parents of adopted children, and stepfamilies, which space does not permit us to list here.

You can learn about local and regional mothers' groups by contacting your library, Family Support America, or the National Self-Help Clearinghouse. Extremely local neighborhood groups can often be found through your YM/WCA, JCC, community recreation center or park district, hospital or birthing center, churches, temples, and children's bookstores.

Family Support America

Formerly known as Family Resource Coalition of America, Family Support America is an umbrella agency of parents' support organizations throughout the United States and Canada. This organization has a national information clearinghouse that lists more than one thousand family service programs. These programs focus on encouraging healthy families by giving parents education and supporting them through the normal stresses of raising children. The FSA can provide a list of programs in your area and information on developing parent support groups and drop-in centers.

158

Contact: Family Support America, 20 N. Wacker Drive, Suite 1100, Chicago, IL 60606; (312) 338-0900. E-mail: info@familysupportamerica.org. Website: www.familysupportamerica.org.

National Self-Help Clearinghouse

This nonprofit organization was founded in 1976. Its mission is to "facilitate access to self-help groups and to increase the awareness of the importance of mutual support." Visit their website to search The Self-Help Sourcebook Online. The Sourcebook is a free database that includes information on over eight hundred national and international self-help support groups. The Sourcebook includes information on starting local self-help groups and provides opportunities to link with others to develop needed self-help groups.

Contact: National Self-Help Clearinghouse, Graduate School and University Center of the City University of New York, 365 Fifth Avenue, Suite 3300, New York, NY 10016; (212) 817-1822. E-mail: info@selfhelpweb.org. Website: http://mentalhelp.net/selfhelp/.

Online support

Thanks to the enormous popularity of the Internet, you don't have to leave the house to find support anymore. Women have been quick to embrace this medium. A milestone was reached in February 2000, when the number of women online surpassed the number of men. At-home mothers have learned that they can combat isolation and communicate with other mothers throughout the world by using e-mail, discussion loops and message boards.

You can chat with other at-home mothers, make new or keep up with old friends, learn about child development, keep current in your professional field, take online classes to pursue a new interest, AND find the perfect stroller through dozens of popular websites, many of which cater specifically to parents. In addition to the mothers' organizations' websites listed earlier in this chapter, the following sites offer up-to-date information and support for both new and seasoned moms:

- www.homeparents.about.com/parenting/homeparents/ (About.com's Guide for Stay-at-Home Parents)
- www.thecybermom.com
- www.localmom.com
- www.MainStreetMom.com
- www.miserlymoms.com
- www.mom.com
- www.MomsOnline.com
- www.myria.com
- www.parenthoodweb.com
- www.ParentSoup.com
- www.parentsplace.com
- www.Salon.com/mwt/ ("Mothers Who Think" column)
- www.storknet.com
- www.wahm.com (for work-at-home moms)

Networking among mothers is a growth area, and new resources and organizations are coming online almost continuously! In an effort to keep our readers as current as possible, Spencer & Waters, the publisher of *Staying Home*, makes available a regularly updated webpage of resources that can be downloaded for free.

Please visit us at www.spencerandwaters.com to get the most up-to-date information for at-home mothers.

Looking Ahead: Taking the
Next Step in
Your Family
Life Cycle

9

Public Networking: Influencing Public Policy on Families, Work Life, and Child Care

We [at-home mothers] need an advocate to ask, where is our retirement plan, our pension? What is Social Security crediting us for all these years at home?
— Nancy Menefee Jackson, *journalist and at-home mother of two daughters*

This chapter addresses in more depth a theme introduced earlier: women tend to see their problems as personal when, in fact, they are social. This is why one cannot be a concerned parent without being interested in public policy issues concerning work and family life. While the work of women outside and inside the home is essential to our economy and quality of life, and while every politician and business leader gives lip service to being pro-family and pro-women, the actual state of affairs doesn't reflect that ethic. Very few of our political, social, or economic institutions have policies or practices that encourage the balanced integration of family life and work life or provide a variety of options so that women and men can make choices that suit their own needs and circumstances.

Recently numerous state and federal legislatures have spent a lot of time and energy working on necessary child-care and parental leave bills to accommodate employed mothers. While such bills are certainly a step in the right direction, legislators have ignored their most numerous single constituency of full-time child-care workers: at-home mothers. These women have many serious questions about current inequitable social and business practices:

- "Why," these mothers ask, "do working parents get tax credits and pretax vouchers for child care while my family does not? After all, my family is the one trying to do without one paycheck."
- "Why," they ask, "if we are committed to women's participation in the work force, wasn't my job protected by federal mandate when I tried to take maternity leave? And why is a six-week leave considered an adequate amount of time for a mother and baby to get to know each other?"
- "Why didn't my husband get the chance to take a parental leave when our child was born?"
- "Why did my former employers spend all that money training me for the electronic age, then reject my offer to take a computer and a modem home to continue working for them?"
- "Why does the government keep telling me it's profamily while actually making it more expensive to have children by refusing to adjust the dependent tax exemption to keep up with inflation?" (If it had kept pace with inflation since the 1950s, the exemption would be worth well over $7,800 per child in today's economy.)
- "Why do merchants keep trying to get my business but provide so few amenities for parents with children, such as changing tables and play corners?"
- "Why does my husband's employer allow him company time to organize a United Way drive or speak at schools to other people's children but frowns on his taking an afternoon off to see our son in a class play?"

Why indeed?

The answers to these questions lie in our society's assumptions about work life and family life. Many of those assumptions are based on the expectation that one parent — the father — will devote himself fully to corporate life, while the other — the mother — will devote herself exclusively to home life. It's as if competition and nurturance have been arbitrarily divided up and assigned gender differences and people are expected to participate fully in one or the other. If you are a worker, both business and government assume that you are concentrating exclusively on that, while someone else takes care of the home. Business and government have programs and policies to help you work, but not ones that help you work and live.

Although there are signs of a growing awareness that work and family issues are interrelated, especially in larger companies, implementation of family-friendly policies — such as job sharing, on-site child care, professional part-time work, flextime, and parental (as opposed to simply maternal) leave — lags far behind. For example, among the 188 U.S. companies surveyed by the Families and Work Institute, only 2 percent have achieved what the institute calls "Stage 3," where work/family issues are integrated into the corporate culture and there is a true commitment to change. One-third of the companies are "barely aware," and 46 percent still view work/family issues as women's problems that do not affect the work force or corporate culture as a whole.[1]

Researcher Felice Schwartz, notorious for sparking public discussion about "the mommy track," suggests that these assumptions persist because they are very real to the male chief executives and politicians who run most companies and hold most political offices. Many of them got where they are, she notes, by sacrificing relationships with their own families. Now they aren't ready to hear that "those who succeed them should go to all the Little League games that they themselves missed."[2] The most inequitable part of this situation is that many top executives think nothing of taking an afternoon off to play golf with a client or keeping in touch with the office electronically via fax and modem while away on a trip, but they wouldn't dream of extending the same flexibility to a lower-level employee — especially a female employee — in the name of improved work/family life balance.

Companies that rigidly subscribe to such an old-fashioned

work model may be in trouble, because Americans' attitudes about their goals and desires are changing. In a 1991 study conducted by the University of Maryland, half of the people polled said they would sacrifice a day's pay for an extra day off each week. Given a choice of eight goals for the future, more than 75 percent said that their top priority was to spend more time with family and friends.[3]

Protests that such radical changes in the work ethic will cause the United States to lose its competitive edge are unfounded. In 1990 the average German worker put in a twenty-nine-hour week, down from a forty-hour average in 1960. Germans also get a standard six weeks of paid vacation. This schedule hasn't adversely affected Germany's competitiveness. In that same year Germany overtook the United States as the world's largest exporter and ranked second behind Japan in worker productivity.

Women with children aren't the only workers who are frustrated with the current American work model. Men also struggle with trying to enjoy their families and live up to corporate expectations. A Du Pont survey of 8,500 of its workers — 70 percent of them men — showed that 56 percent of the men were interested in flexible work hours, up from 37 percent five years earlier.[4]

Sometimes, people don't even realize that they are frustrated until a new option becomes available to them. In 1989 Philip Haebler, a manager with a very large restaurant chain, lost his job and became a consultant. He took a 50 percent cut in salary and switched from a BMW to a station wagon, but the trade-off was well worth it. He now spends much more time with his three children. "I used to be on the train to work before they were even awake," he recalled in an interview, "but now I can get them off to school. And I have memories I never would have had — like seeing my daughter's face light up when I meet her at the school bus."[5] Recently, Haebler was offered a new corporate job that would have doubled his income — and his time commitments. He turned it down. "It wasn't worth it to me," he said.

Haebler was able to find a new, better model of work and family life, but he had to do it on his own, and he had to work against assumptions of what a working father should value. What assumptions do other countries make?

Most other industrialized societies assume that all parents, whatever work they do, deserve some assistance and consideration from their government. In recent years many articles have called Americans' attention to the widely subsidized day-care systems of European countries, but few of these articles stress the point that European policies and practices help all parents, not just "working" parents. European policies accommodate the needs of at-home parents by offering more options, subsidizing families who wish to keep a parent at home until the children start school, and protecting those parents who choose to stay home from unfair career and benefit penalties.

For example, the French system of free public preschools for three- to six-year-olds, called Ecole Maternelles, is used by 95 percent of French families, whether or not one parent is home full-time. Since day care is subsidized by the government, not individual companies, its accessibility and low cost open it up to all mothers. At-home mothers also like to use these Ecole Maternelles for play and socialization opportunities for their children and as a break for themselves, especially if they have a younger child at home.

In Hungary parental leave can extend to as much as three years, with a generous 75 percent of wage replacement for about half of that time period. Some mothers and fathers return to work when the wage replacement runs out; others choose to scrape along on a reduced budget for the full three years, at which time the children become eligible for preschool. When the parents return to work, they return to their regular pay scale. In Sweden parents have the right to work a reduced-hour day (with adjusted pay) until the child is eight years old. In Austria and several other countries families receive a monthly child-care stipend from the government.

In almost all other European countries mothers and fathers can put together a combination of paid and unpaid leave to spend at least the first critical year at home with their child, have access to subsidized alternative child care, and can arrange for part-time work or reduced hours. All these countries have decided that child care and family life are as important to the national well-being as, say, oil drilling and bombs. They have funded programs accordingly, without putting unfair burdens on small businesses, individual counties, or urban versus rural areas. Through the allocation of government funds, they have sent a clear message about their priorities.

How does the United States compare? Not very well. In contrast to their European counterparts, American parents, and American women in particular, do not seem to get much back from their government in the way of services and entitlements (see the chart on page 170–171).

Author Sylvia Anne Hewlett offers a critical analysis of this issue in *A Lesser Life: The Myth of Women's Liberation in America.* Hewlett points out that in this country, "we have not yet created a context that allows a woman to reasonably expect that she can have both a career and a family. . . . The Europeans got it right when they decided to push not only for equal rights in the sphere of work but also for social benefits to ease the family responsibilities of working women. . . . The United States does less than any other advanced country to make life easier for working mothers."[6] This also applies to working fathers who want to divide their time between career and family.

Why, you may ask, are we paying such close attention to child-care policies? After all, at-home mothers care for their own children by themselves and don't need any help — right?

Wrong. Although child care takes place in your home, you and your family still live in a social context. We take child-care policies very seriously for two reasons.

First, these policies indicate how seriously a society takes child care — whether it acknowledges that the work mothers do with children is important and whether this work is invisible or considered worthy of national attention. They are a key indicator of the true status of women and children in the society.

Second, as our survey and interviews made clear, all parents, including working and at-home mothers, are passionately interested in a wider array of options. Working mothers fantasize about more time with their kids; at-home mothers dream about part-time or reduced-hours professional work. As Lili Hartman, a New Jersey program director who has been at home for five years with her two children, put it, "What would be great is if there was such a thing in this country as meaningful, well-paid part-time work so that we could have a balance in our lives. That's what most women I know want."

Women who desire this balance are not having outrageous hallucinations. In France or Sweden such dreams are a reality. In fact, as the chart on page 170–171 shows, most European countries have responded to their citizens' desires by implementing national policies that help them achieve that kind of balance.

In addition, at some point in their careers as parents, many mothers will need an alternative child-care arrangement due to divorce, disability, finances, or a change in personal goals. Or a family disaster may send them back into the work force with savage swiftness.

This is why public policy issues concerning work and family life should be on the professional agenda of every parent, whether they work outside the home or not. The range of issues is very wide. They may be corporate concerns, such as parental leave, flextime, or on-site day care; or they may reach into the home, as in the case of child-care tax credits and restrictions on home-based businesses; or they may be issues that essentially involve the community, such as tot lots or changing tables in libraries and public buildings.

Corporate Change

Increasingly, parents are telling employers that they will do the same work in fewer hours or less work for less money — take it or leave it. Companies eventually will have to take note because demographics are on the parents' side. As the work force dwindles and becomes proportionally more female in the twenty-first century, the competition among companies for good workers will heat up. Employee retention will become critical. Employers will have to take note of working parents' needs or risk losing valuable employees.

Providing flexible work and family benefits can help the corporations, too. A recent analysis of eighty research studies found that companies that help employees balance work and family have reduced turnover, less absenteeism, and increased productivity.[7] The rigid males-only work ethic may finally change under demo-

The Big Picture

Country	Percent of Women with Children Under 6 in Labor Force	Length of Paid Job-Protected Leave	Percent of Wage Replaced
Finland	75%	10½ months, including 1 month before birth	80%
France	60%	16 weeks, including 6 weeks before birth	90%
West Germany	50%	14 weeks, including 6 weeks before birth	90%
Hungary	80%	24 weeks, including 4 weeks before birth	65–100% depending on prior work history
Italy	45%	5 months, including 2 months before birth	80%
Sweden	80%	15 months	1 year at 90%; 3 months at low flat rate
United States	57%	No national policy	No national policy

Sheila B. Kamerman, Professor of Social Policy and Planning, The Columbia University School Social Work, *Working Mother,* September 1990, p. 67.

Available to Fathers	Additional Benefits	Percent of Children Under 3 in Part- and Full-Time Care	Percent of Children 3–6 in Part- and Full-Time Care
Last 6 months	Job-protected leave until child is 3, paid at lower level; four days annual paid sick-child leave	67% of 2-year-olds and 33% of 1-year-olds	70%
No	2-year unpaid parental leave for either parent; modest cash benefit for low-income families	45% of 2-year-olds; 10–15% of under 2s	97%
No	18 months modest cash benefits	Under 5%	80%
No	For those who qualify, following 24 weeks, 75% of wages until child is 1½, then modest cash benefits; sick-child leave also	10–20%	85–90%
Partly	1 year unpaid job-protected leave	5–10%	75%
Yes	3 additional months unpaid job-protected leave; right to work 6-hour day until child is 8; sick-child leave	76% for all ages 1–6	—
No	Where paid disability leave is available, it must apply to pregnancy and maternity; about half of all states require unpaid job-protected leave	20%	70%

graphic pressure and with the right kinds of benefit demands from parents.

The good news is that some changes are already happening. IBM and other major corporations offer a child-care referral service; Johnson & Johnson provides yearlong family-care leaves. On-site day-care centers are beginning to appear at companies such as Johnson & Johnson, Prudential, Dun & Bradstreet, Neilsen & Company, and American Bankers Insurance Group. The concept of a parental leave for either the mother or the father (or leaves that can be sequenced back-to-back) also is gaining popularity.

On the other hand, some family programs developed by businesses can actually be counterproductive for employees. For instance, one new mother who was struggling with the decision to stay home or return to work opted for returning to the office when her company opened an on-site day-care center. Six months later she was struggling with an unexpected side effect: workaholism. The on-site center has changed the corporate culture to encourage longer hours, as the center is open to 8 P.M. and on weekends. Since her husband also stays late at his office, and with no incentive for either of them to leave work on time, they now have less family time than ever before.

Another mother was very pleased to have negotiated a four-day workweek with her company — even though she took a cut in pay while carrying the same work load (made possible by longer hours and working at home). Like many mothers, she felt the company was doing her a favor by taking her back and had to negotiate from a position of weakness, not strength.

One manager who works for a large international benefits and compensation consulting firm commented, "Most family benefits that corporations offer are actually targeted at getting employees to work even more and spend less time with their families." This manager's firm encourages its employees to spend long hours in the office by offering free food in the cafeteria all day long. A dedicated employee can eat breakfast, lunch, and dinner on the job. The firm also pays free overnight dependent care for consultants who need to take frequent business trips. While this is ostensibly a nice benefit, it also makes it much harder for parents who don't want to be on the road that often.

It pays not to take all the "family-friendly" benefits offered by corporations at face value. Are they benefits that truly accommodate family life, or are they simply quick fixes that keep all the worker bees focused on corporate responsibilities to the exclusion of other ties?

To familiarize yourself with the range of programs offered and for more information on some of the better companies to work for, consult *Companies That Care,* by Hal Morgan and Kerry Tucker (Fireside, Simon & Schuster, 1991). The authors surveyed major corporations on their family policies and include information on child care, elder care, and workplace flexibility. *The Corporate Reference Guide to Work-Family Programs*, by the Families and Work Institute, which evaluates the quality and degree of corporate family friendliness, also is a valuable source.

Societal Change

Change is taking place in individual companies, but to truly protect and serve all parents, change needs to be part of national policy, as in Europe. Your individual rights and entitlements should not be subject to the whim of your employer. The 1991 National Commission on Children acknowledged the economic inequalities caused by inadequate tax exemptions when it recommended a universal $1,000 per child tax credit for all parents.[8] At first glance, this recommendation seems promising, until you realize that family advocates have been making similar recommendations for twenty years — none of which have been implemented.

Over two decades ago, the 1970 White House Conference on Children made many of the same recommendations, including a call for more flextime and part-time work. In addition, the conference recommended that part-time work be "upgraded in status, so that parents could give time to parenting without totally sacrificing their careers and opportunities for advancement."

Today federal and university commissions continue to report

173

on the same needs and act as if their findings are new. Their findings are not new. While we continue to perform studies, Europe implements changes.

We don't need more research.[9] There is, in fact, a remarkable consensus among family advocates on what is needed: parental leave, job security, national health insurance not tied to any one job, flextime, professional part-time work, job sharing, and subsidized child care — whether that care is being given by a parent or another provider.

What is needed to effect these changes? What is needed is what has always worked when the need for society-wide changes became clear — good old-fashioned American activism. The time for research is over. The time for national and grass roots efforts is now.

We need activism because, despite the positive changes on the corporate and national fronts, changes are not happening fast enough, with enough continuity, or through enough sectors of society. What can you do? The next section provides some suggestions.

Getting Involved

The first thing you should understand is that as a professional, your talents and business world expertise will be in great demand. A wide variety of associations and organizations provide the opportunity to become involved with public policy issues that are of interest to you. A trip to your local library to review the latest edition of the *Encyclopedia of Associations* will provide brief synopses and contact addresses for hundreds of business, trade, government, scientific, educational, cultural, religious, athletic, and public affairs organizations. Some, like NOW, have women's issues as their primary focus. Others, like the American Civil Liberties Union (ACLU), have special-interest standing committees. Still others, like the Homemakers' Coalition for Equal Rights, work specifically to improve the legal, economic, and social position of at-home mothers and homemakers.

As a way of keeping connected to your former career, you may decide to work through a professional or trade association to which you already belong. If you have a very strong interest in a specific issue, such as national parental leave or increasing the dependent tax exemption, you will probably want to investigate several groups until you find one that has an active program in that area. For instance, OWL, the Older Women's League (730 11th Street, NW, Washington, DC 20001), is nationally known for being very active on issues such as pensions and full Social Security benefits for women whose careers have been interrupted. If you are interested in these issues, you may want to contact OWL, even if you are only in your twenties or thirties.

Sometimes newspaper and magazine articles on current public policies mention groups that are actively lobbying on an issue. These, too, can be good sources for organizations you might want to join.

On a personal level, getting involved in national public policy can be very rewarding. Columnist Joyce Maynard has written that she used to think that being a mother and taking good care of her children was reason enough not to be an actively involved citizen, but she has come to see that "there is no way to be a good mother without also looking out for the world one's children will someday inherit."[10]

Getting involved in public policy issues often can be done on a flexible schedule that accommodates your other responsibilities. Your involvement may mean long-term service on an organization's standing committee, occasional participation in a fund-raising or letter-writing campaign, or short-term intensive research for a position paper. Usually you have the opportunity to choose to work on issues of specific interest to you — something we don't always get in an office environment.

Former career skills, whether they be technical or interpersonal, usually have direct transfer value for political action. For some women, such as the former hospital publicist who edits a newsletter for a group campaigning for national health care, it means using the skills you already have. For others, such as the shy suburban bookkeeper, it may mean developing new interpersonal skills by conducting a door-to-door survey on discriminatory Social Security policies for your local NOW chapter.

In many cases, immediate results and benefits can be achieved by following the slogan of the environmental movement: "Think globally, act locally." Local efforts can have extraordinary results in an astonishingly short time, especially when they focus on direct action items — that is, requests to implement very specific and identifiable changes — as opposed to mere policy statements. Voting for or against a specific bill (such as the Caregivers Act, sponsored by Mary Rose Oakar of Ohio, which would credit care giving for Social Security benefits), funding a local day-care center, putting changing tables in washrooms at the local library, and implementing a flextime schedule are direct action items. These are the specific things you ask politicians and industry to do to back up their vague policy statements regarding how "pro-women" or "pro-family" they are.

For example, one Illinois mother of two preschoolers got exasperated at her local copy shop. She went there several times a week to make photocopies for her local mothers' organization and had to try to keep her two bored children from wreaking havoc in the store while she was making her copies. She finally suggested to the manager that the store offer a toy center where children could play while parents used their services. She told him that she felt this move would bring in more parental business. When she walked into the store the next week, she was surprised and gratified to find a comfortable, toy-filled play area ready to use.

Local action also can have a profound national influence, as shown by the success story of Action for Children's Television (ACT), a consumer group formed by concerned Boston-area mothers in 1968. Their story, told here by founder Peggy Charren, is a case study of how to conduct an effective special-interest campaign with tremendous national impact.

> When we got started, I had a three-year-old child, and my older child was eight. What I saw on TV for children was terrible — there wasn't much of anything for small children to watch, except for wall-to-wall monster cartoons. Television could surely be put to better use.

I figured I had two years in which to fix it because when my younger daughter was five I would go back to work, and in those two years what a nice volunteer effort that would be, to change children's television so that it was more responsive to the needs of children. I called a group of friends over to the house, and, naïve as it sounds to me saying it out loud right now, I felt that a little output on my part and some friends was going to change a multibillion-dollar industry. But I think that consumer activists have to think that their effort is going to make change — otherwise you're going to have no energy to go on. And certainly, if nothing else I had learned patience after eight years as a parent.

After two or three months our group dwindled to four or five women — all of us had young children, and all of us had worked but were not then working outside the home. And I think that is the essential ingredient to the start of ACT. I think the fact that we had work experience was important. We tended to see this as a professional effort from the minute we started. We wanted to organize in a way different from just sitting together and talking. We were very much aware of what you do to start an organization; you name it, you incorporate, you have limited liability.

We also made sure to get our facts straight, to educate ourselves on what the problem really was. One of the first things we did was subscribe to all the industry magazines, so we could see what the other side was thinking. The pressure has to look like it comes from a group that knows how to put pressure on all the parts of society that might make change; otherwise the broadcaster wasn't going to pay attention.

We called up the local broadcasters to make appointments to ask them why they thought this was what they should be doing for children. And it was actually the answers of the broadcasters that gave ACT its modus operandi for the last ten years. They were very honest — they said that the reason why television for children lacked diversity and doesn't seem to be very creative or exciting is because that's how it gets the largest

177

share of the two- to eleven-year-old market! To hear your child referred to as part of the two- to eleven-year-old market was a shock. But it was honest. That was exactly how the broadcaster thought of children. And for this reason ACT took the position that what we would try to do is eliminate advertising on children's television.

At that point we did a whole lot of research. For example, we discovered that a show for preschoolers turned out to be 70 percent commercials. They used to put blindfolds on the kids' eyes and had them reach out to touch and guess. Well, in this program what the kids touch was a toy that was being advertised. So that the program content was also commercial. That was an eye-opener!

We knew that the Federal Communications Commission was the prime organization responsible for making rules about broadcasting, so we decided that we had to go to the commission. And people said, "How on earth did you get in to see the commissioner? What did you do to get to see the commissioner?" The answer is, we called him up on the phone and asked, "Can we come down to see you?" and he said yes. I think in retrospect, if we had known that no group had done that before, we might have thought twice about it. But not knowing that, calling up seemed like the most direct way to handle the problem, and it worked.

So we presented a petition to the F.C.C. to eliminate advertising from children's television. We feel eliminating advertising would have to improve the quality of the programming for children because the networks would no longer feel compelled to compete for "the larger share of the two- to eleven-year-old market."

In the course of eight years we've managed to reduce the amount of advertising by 40 percent on the weekends and we've gotten rid of hosts doing commercials.[11]

Why was ACT so successful? First, the members took themselves and their issue seriously. Second, they conducted themselves professionally and took the time to solidify a core group and conduct their research, then identified and analyzed their problem. Finally, they zeroed in on a specific solution to a specific problem and targeted the best possible agent of that change for their petitioning process.

Local groups also can use their influence effectively by petitioning elected representatives. Andrea Camp, an experienced aide to longtime women's advocate Representative Pat Schroeder of Colorado, recommends that you "organize ten or fifteen people and ask to meet with your congressperson in the home district."

Meeting with your local legislator is easier than you may think. Get together with your mothers' group, food co-op, or neighborhood association and write to request a meeting on your group's letterhead. The purpose of this audience with your senator or congressional representative is not only to get his or her views on family issues but also to inform him or her of your own. Come prepared with your background information and a short list of action items from your group. Present your ideas much as you would present a proposal to a client or another department in your business.

Be prepared to answer questions about your group's purpose and why you have a special interest in this particular public policy issue. Be prepared to ask your representative where he or she stands on whichever issue you have targeted: national health and child care, national parental leave entitlement, nondiscriminatory Social Security benefits for workers with interrupted careers, raising dependent tax exemptions, or another issue of concern to parents. If his or her views do not represent yours, get back to him or her with a well-researched position paper signed by other groups or a community petition. Don't give up on your representative until the next election, when you can voice your opinion with your vote.

If your schedule doesn't permit you to see your representative in person, consider using a letter-writing campaign instead. Elected officials do keep track of their correspondence, and even as few as ten or fifteen letters on the same subject will get their attention. For parents of preschoolers, a campaign of this type (consisting of a form letter or position paper on a specific topic sent by numerous people to your representative and to the local newspaper) may be much more feasible. Your letter campaign will have the greatest impact if it is on an issue either currently or soon to be up for debate in Congress.

To have the most impact on changing our society's and business community's treatment of families, parents of all political persuasions and backgrounds need to band together to get their voices heard. Whether you have the personnel and resources to start your own small group or prefer working with an established organization is entirely up to you. Your choice may be based on proximity and schedule as much as personality!

The important thing is to get involved in changing the way our society views the relationship between work and family life and to extend the number of options women and men have to help balance their careers as professionals and as committed parents. Feminist Anita Shreve writes, "At issue today is nothing less than the very nature of work and love, and the opportunity for women to have both in their lives."[12]

Following is a list of some of the better-known national advocacy groups. For more information on local groups, consult your local Republican or Democrat party committee, the United Way, the YMCA or YWCA, and local affiliates and chapters of these national groups. Also consult our list of at-home mothers' organizations in Chapter 8. Mothers at Home and FEMALE, in particular, have task forces concerned with changing societal perceptions and public policies on families with mothers at home.

American Association of University Women
2401 Virginia Avenue, NW
Washington, DC 20037
(202) 785-7700
Open to all women with college degrees; seeks to advance the status of women, especially in education and employment.

American Civil Liberties Union
22 E. 40th Street
New York, NY 10016
(212) 725-1222

Association of Part-Time Professionals
7700 Leesburg Pike
Crescent Plaza, Suite 216
Falls Church, VA 22043
(703) 734-7975
Promotes employment opportunities for men and women interested in part-time professional work and aims to upgrade the status of part-time employment.

B'nai B'rith
1640 Rhode Island Avenue, NW

Washington, DC 20036
(202) 857-6655
National organization of Jewish women lobbies in Washington; also active locally on women's issues.

Children's Defense Fund
122 C Street, NW
Washington, DC 20001
(202) 628-8787
National group that advocates for children's rights in public policy through research, education, litigation, and legislation.

Church Women United
475 Riverside Drive
New York, NY 10015
(212) 870-2347
Peace and women's rights advocacy group.

Coalition of Labor Union Women
15 Union Square
New York, NY 10003
(212) 242-0700
Promotes equal opportunities for women and encourages participation of union women in politics.

Congressional Caucus for
Women's Issues
2471 Rayburn House Office
Building
Washington, DC 20515
(202) 225-6740
Works to promote women's issues through the national legislative process.

Displaced Homemakers Network
1411 K Street, NW
Washington, DC 20005
(202) 628-6767
Provides technical assistance and public information about the pro-

grams and services available to displaced homemakers.

Homemakers' Coalition for Equal
Rights
Alice Dyson
403 Bryant
Glen Ellyn, IL 60137
Seeks to improve the legal, economic, and social position of the homemaker.

Homeworkers Organized for More
Employment
P.O. Box 10
Orland, ME 04472
(207) 469-7961
Since 1970 this organization for home craft workers has provided catalog outlets, information, and support; publishes a quarterly newsletter.

Institute for American Values
250 W. 57th Street
New York, NY 10107
(212) 246-3942
This nonpartisan, nonprofit policy organization is concerned with issues affecting the well-being of the American family and is working to establish a national family agenda; publishes a newsletter, Family Affairs.

League of Women Voters
1730 M Street, NW
Washington, DC 20006
(202) 429-1965
Nonpartisan organization that promotes political responsibility and informed participation for all citizens; conducts registration drives, initiates candidate forums, sponsors the presidential debates, and lobbies on a wide variety of local and national issues.

181

National Federation of Business and Professional Women's Clubs, Inc.
2012 Massachusetts Avenue, NW
Washington, DC 20036
(202) 293-1100
Since 1919 this 125,000-member organization for working women has promoted the interests of women. It advocates legislative changes to secure equal rights, encourages corporate/private sector responsiveness to the needs of working women on issues such as dependent care, and works through numerous local affiliates. A bimonthly tabloid keeps members up-to-date on socioeconomic issues such as pay equity and child care.

National Organization for Women
1000 16th Street, NW
Washington, DC 20036
(202) 331-0066
National membership organization with numerous local affiliates; participates in political, legislative, and public educational activities designed to promote women's equality. NOW Legislative Office: 1266 National Press Building, Washington, DC 20004; (202) 347-2279.

National Women's Political Caucus
1275 K Street, NW
Washington, DC 20005
(202) 898-1100
Founded in 1971 as a multipartisan vehicle to move women into public office, the NWPC currently has about 75,000 members; lobbies on reproductive rights and issues of comparable worth; raises money for Democratic and Republican party women candidates to encourage an equal

voice and place for women in the political process at all levels. Quarterly newsletter.

Network
806 Rhode Island Avenue, NE
Washington, DC 20018
(202) 526-4070
Catholic laity and other religious persons of all faiths who lobby for national legislation on behalf of the poor and powerless on a variety of economic and social issues.

New Ways to Work
149 Ninth Street
San Francisco, CA 94103
(415) 552-1000
Since 1972 has provided information, training, and support to individuals and organizations interested in new work options such as flextime, job sharing, and reduced work time; publishes a newsletter and offers technical assistance to employers and unions contemplating new work options.

9 to 5: National Association of Working Women
614 Superior Avenue, NW
Cleveland, OH 44113
(216) 566-9308
National organization for women office workers with numerous local chapters. Seeks to improve the working conditions of women, provides public information on the status and concerns of working women, and promotes their interests through lobbying and political activities. Produces studies in areas such as hazards of video display terminals, automation, and family and medical leave. Bimonthly newsletter.

Parent Action
2 Hopkins Plaza
Baltimore, MD 21201
(410) 752-1790
National membership organization dedicated to speaking out for what parents need. Founded by child-care expert T. Berry Brazelton. Publishes the Parent Post *newsletter.*

Women Employed
22 W. Monroe Street
Chicago, IL 60603
(312) 782-3902
Since 1973 this organization has helped women improve job opportunities. Conducts advocacy efforts on pay equity, parental leave, and non-traditional jobs for women; analyzes government programs and employer

policies that affect women; and develops recommendations for public and corporate policy changes.

Women's Legal Defense Fund
1875 Connecticut Avenue, NW
Washington, DC 20009
(202) 986-2600
Since 1971 this 18,000-member organization of attorneys, paralegals, administrators, publicists, and secretaries has promoted legal rights for women through litigation, advocacy, and counseling. Works for women's rights in family law, employment, and education; provides telephone referrals and counseling on credit discrimination, domestic relations, and employment discrimination. Publishes handbooks and manuals.

10

Options: Community Work, Home-Based Businesses, and Reentering the Outside Work Force

I'll never work forty hours a week again. There's no way I'll punch a time clock. I'm looking for something more flexible to do.
— Pat Ricono, *at-home mother of three sons*

Today, at-home motherhood is usually not a lifetime proposition. While a woman's childbearing years in the nineteenth or early twentieth century might have spanned thirty years, women today tend to raise children in a much narrower time frame. With an average life expectancy of seventy-eight years, today's woman is looking at spending a significantly smaller proportion of her life caring for children than her mother or grandmother did. Even mothers who nurture their children all the way to adulthood eventually will be left with an empty nest. Whether it's after a few months or several years, most women find that at some point they're ready to increase their involvement outside the home.

Although going back to paid work is certainly an option, it's not the only choice open to you. After so many years of being "on call," some women enjoy being "retired" and finally having time to pursue their personal interests and hobbies. Community work is an equally valid choice; many women find a great deal of satisfaction in contributing their skills to their community, their church or temple, or their children's schools.

Others find that a home-based business or flexible work is more rewarding than going back to a nine-to-five job. In this chapter, we look at all the options open to you and explore how to go about deciding when you're ready to return to the work force.

Sequencing

Arlene Rossen Cardozo's ground-breaking book *Sequencing* was published in 1986, introducing a new word and new concept into the public domain. Cardozo argues persuasively that the prevailing model of the supermother is destructive. She proposes an alternative called sequencing, which involves "having it all, but not all at once."[1] In Cardozo's view, it makes much more sense for a woman to have a balanced life by concentrating her energies on one stage at a time instead of doing a juggling act. She suggests a three-step approach: (1) establishing your career, (2) staying home to raise your children, and (3) finding ways to continue work and family as your children grow.

Most of the mothers we interviewed embrace this idea and feel that staying home with young children is one part of a full life. In fact, leaving your job to pursue other opportunities — whether to be home with your children or to pursue an entirely different career — is now much more common among both men and women than spending all of your working years at the same company. Child-care authority Penelope Leach notes that the pattern of emerging from school or college onto the bottom rung of a ladder and then climbing as fast and as high as you can before retirement knocks you off is already outdated. "Most of us," she writes, "will have to train and re-train several times and that will mean that an adult working life divides into chunks. One of these chunks could be parenthood. A stage of life when you — and society — accepted that your priority was your family and that for this time your career or your job took second place."[2]

It's reassuring to many women at home that sequencing is already a tested concept that has worked for women of our mothers' generation. Supreme Court Justice Sandra Day O'Connor and former U.N. ambassador Jeane Kirkpatrick are two prominent examples of women who took time out from their careers to have children and went on to enjoy great success in a wider sphere.

The owner of a thriving public relations firm told us, "I know of many women in their fifties who didn't launch their careers until they were in their forties. I was out of the work force for eleven years and then successfully started my own business. Many women have bought into the idea that if you leave the work force for a while to raise your children, your career is irretrievably damaged. The truth is, if you're good, there will always be a place for you. It's nonsense that you can never catch up if you take some time off."

Other sequencing parents say that while you can achieve tremendous success in your career, it is unrealistic to assume that you will accelerate at the same pace as a contemporary whose work pattern is uninterrupted. One sociologist who returned to teach at her university after spending ten years at home with her kids notes that all of her contemporaries already have tenure, but she does not. She admits that she works harder now and tries to publish more to make up for lost time. Her work is going well, and she is pretty sure that eventually she will reach her goal — albeit a decade or more after her fellow graduates. This mother still expects to achieve great things in her field; she has simply pushed back her "achievement deadline."

It also is true that the longer you work, the more chance you will have to recoup from taking time off. With the mandatory retirement age being pushed back farther and farther, chances are good that you could devote twenty years to your children and still have twenty productive years in the paid work force.

There are, however, financial penalties for sequencing. Under our country's current system, there are rewards for staying in the work force beyond a monthly income. For example, you can command a higher salary, contribute more to a pension fund (though an encouraging trend is that the minimum number of years it takes to be vested in a plan is coming down to as few as five), have a fully deductible IRA, and eventually reap more Social Security benefits after you retire.

Some of these penalties, such as reduced IRA and Social Security eligibility, may be changed at the federal level (see Chapter 9). Others, such as company-specific pension requirements, promotional procedures, and age discrimination, may change under demographic pressure as companies have to compete harder for a reduced pool of workers in the twenty-first century.

No matter what penalties may exist, thousands of parents believe that the trade-off is worth the opportunity for a balanced life that sequencing affords them. There are many successful sequencing stories, and all share certain patterns. Women who are most successful at resuming an outside career are those who (1) keep their hand in their careers during the at-home years by maintaining contact with former coworkers and employers, reading professional journals, attending conferences or classes, or doing occasional freelance work; (2) show creativity in finding or developing work opportunities that can be done part-time or at home; (3) have support for their endeavors — both moral and practical — from family members and friends; and (4) have the determination to achieve both meaningful time with their children and time for their careers.

Although sequencing is an important concept for at-home mothers, some women question Cardozo's emphasis on returning to paid work in stage three. Although Cardozo does mention community work,[3] she implies that resuming a paid career is the inevitable culmination of a woman's time at home. Certainly, women who choose to donate their time to nonprofit, political, or civic organizations are just as productive as those who return to full-time employment.

Taking Part in Community Work

Though it's not for everyone, most mothers do engage in some type of community work during their time at home. In fact, the donated labor of skilled women is the hidden engine of the most valued community benefits, such as libraries, social services, schools, park districts, and growth and development programs. If you feel you're ready to participate in community work, there are sure to be dozens of local nonprofit and charitable groups eager for your help. Deciding which one to get involved in may be the hardest part. The possibilities mentioned by the women in our survey include the following:

- being a room mother or aide at your child's school
- serving on the library board or town council
- becoming active in the PTA
- joining a cooperative nursery school
- visiting nursing homes and hospitals
- teaching adults to read through adult literacy programs or taping books for the visually impaired
- collecting money for charities
- getting involved in your church or temple
- running for local office
- taking a leadership role in the scouts or a mothers' group
- organizing fund-raising events
- leading a local art, music, or drama group
- helping with a local food bank or homeless shelter
- volunteering at a recycling center
- reaching out to new neighbors through Welcome Wagon

With all these options to choose from, how do you decide which one is right for you? Some women look for opportunities that will allow them to use their work skills while they're at home. Volunteering can help you keep up with your previous career. "As a nurse," Carol Edson told us, "I missed the patient contact and my professional colleagues once I retired from hospital nursing. I have been able to meet this need by doing four hours of volunteer work per week as a hospice nurse." Other women lend their expertise in accounting, marketing and public relations, management, and personnel administration to a local organization by serving on its board of directors.

Community work may be even more valuable in helping you develop new skills and pursue new interests. If you have always been interested in writing or photography, you can polish your skills by offering to help put a newsletter together or write press releases for a community group. Or you may look for work that allows you to help others and grow yourself. Some women choose to work with teenagers in crisis pregnancy centers or staff suicide hotlines. One den leader for her son's Cub Scout den said this about the work she does with the scouts: "It really challenges my intuition to divine what makes each boy tick, broadens my creativity to devise projects which will use each boy's skills, deepens my nurturing to develop the best in each boy, and stretches my management skills to accomplish all this in two hours each week!"

Sometimes community work can lead a woman in an entirely new direction. Barbara Carter worked as a documentation editor before having twins. After the care of her twins became easier, she started feeling lonely and looked around for something to get involved in. She told us, "My daughters had been in early intervention programs due to prematurity, and I became involved with making a video to help raise money for the center. At one point, I gave a speech before several hundred people. I also became a volunteer phone counselor for the local hospital to talk to other parents of twins and premature infants. I wouldn't have done any of those things if I hadn't stayed home."

An advantage of community work over paid employment is that it is usually more flexible. Often children can come along to help (and learn along with you), and schedules may be flexible enough so that you can fit your volunteer work in around your own tight family requirements. Community work also can increase self-esteem by giving you the feeling that you are making a real contribution to others. Pat Ricono, a mother of three young boys, said she depends on her volunteer work to make her feel that she's accomplishing something during her at-home years. She noted, "You can get recognition there and feel like a superstar."

There are some drawbacks to community work, of course. Not getting paid for all of your efforts is an obvious one. But many savvy women use their community work as a way to gain marketable skills that will help them when they are ready to get back into the work force. Joanne Brundage says, "Volunteer work has been a dirty concept for a number of years, ever since feminists argued that women have given their time and talents for free. It's not giving away work for free. It's getting job training for free. It's a fair trade."[4] Brundage put this belief into practice by founding FEMALE, a national at-home mothers' group, and by serving on the board of her local historical society.

In the process, she told us, "I've learned more on-the-job skills since I've been home than I ever did when I got a paycheck. I was a mail carrier for ten years, and all that taught me was how to avoid getting dog bites and how to dress warm in the winter. Since starting FEMALE, I've learned nitty-gritty stuff like how to lay out, paste up, and produce a newsletter from beginning to end. I've learned organizational skills, though I'm still working on them. I've learned marketing and public relations — I'm now pretty well versed in giving an interview to the media — and I've learned a lot about teamwork and leadership skills. I now have much more confidence that I will be able to find a rewarding paid job when I need or want to."

Another frequent but less discussed problem is that a willing volunteer worker can find herself besieged by organizations asking for her help. Career women bring expertise and experience to institutions that are in desperate need of professional help, and their skills are in considerable demand. Because of this, a sought-after volunteer may spend as much time away from home working on projects as she would if she were in the paid work force. Some mothers can end up feeling exhausted, burned out, and unappreciated when they take on too many commitments.

The solution isn't difficult, but it does take some assertiveness. It's important to say no when you feel you can't comfortably take on another thing in your life. After all, you stayed home primarily to be with your children, not to leave them with a baby-sitter every day while you fulfill your volunteer obligations. If you find that happening, it's best to cut back on some of your outside commitments before you start feeling the effects of too much stress. It also helps to be clear about how much time you are willing to give when you start a new volunteer position and then don't budge when asked to take on more. If you are realistic and set clear limits, you are more likely to enjoy and benefit from your community involvement.

Returning to the Paid Work Force

Although community work has many rewards, at some point you will probably consider taking on a paid position. How do you decide when the time is right for you to step back into the outside work force?

In many ways, you should approach this decision in the same forthright, analytical manner you used to make the decision to stay home (see Chapter 2). Many of the issues — family finances; pressure from husband, family, and friends; and personal desire for achievement — are the same. You also will have to consider the effect on your children's lives, perhaps including saving money for their college education.

For many families, the time is right when the last child enters school. Large blocks of your time will now be freed up on a regular basis. Family and friends often assume that this is the "natural" time for you to reenter the work force, but this is not necessarily so. For some, the beginning of school signals an even more intense involvement with child and community.

One thirty-seven-year-old mother who teaches evening courses at the local university while her husband covers the child-care front was surprised at her own reaction to their daughter's entry into elementary school. "It is ironic," she said, "but now I find myself wanting to spend less time working away from home and more time volunteering at her school. I want to serve on the PTA boards and in general just be very involved in her education. As a result, I actually plan on cutting back my own teaching schedule next year."

A forty-year-old educational reading specialist, currently at home with her two preadolescent children, told us, "I also plan on being home for them when they are in those so-emotional adolescent years. I realize that that time will be just as important as these primary years are now. And as an educator, I have seen how much of a difference Mom being at home can make."

Even if you and your family decide that it makes economic sense for you to be back in a paid job, you may not be ready emotionally to do so. Mothers are often reluctant to give up those

191

extra hours with their children that they've come to cherish. Others worry about whether their time at home will be held against them when they interview for a professional position, especially if they have been at home for more than five years. They wonder whether they'll be taken seriously or patronized and whether they will be able to obtain a position similar to the one they left or will have to start all over again at the bottom.

One mother of a three-year-old son said, "There's always that fear there. How do you explain spending several years at home on your résumé? There may be some discrimination or disapproval on the part of employers. I have an underlying uneasiness about it, but until I try to go back to work, I won't know how hard it will be."

Some women we surveyed are confident of their skills but concerned about their age when they reenter the work force. One woman who has been home for twelve years raising three children commented, "The only thing I'm concerned about is the factor of my age, not my experience or competence. If I start a new career at age forty-five, say, people might see me as slow to learn or set in my ways. This is a stereotype about age, not just about women."

To combat employers' misconceptions about at-home mothers, apply *Ground rule number 2: Acknowledge your skills.* Not only do you still have the skills you developed in your previous paid position, but you also have gained a host of new abilities and talents since you've been at home. Eleanor Berman, in her encouraging book *Re-Entering: Successful Back-to-Work Strategies for Women Seeking a Fresh Start,* remarks that mothers at home "have been enrolled in one of the best, most demanding management training programs in the world."[5] Mothers learn valuable skills such as time management, problem solving, handling distractions, decision making, and balancing the needs of different children with different personalities. As Berman points out, all these traits are directly translatable into work force success.

Other skills that at-home mothers hone include supervising, communicating, organizing, counseling, educating, planning, budgeting, and negotiating. One woman entrepreneur commented, "If you can figure out which one gets the gumdrop, the 4-year-old or the 6-year-old, you can negotiate any contract in the world."[6]

Women in the helping professions have found that their mothering experience has been especially beneficial when they return to paid employment. Heidi Heinrichs, a nurse with two young children, told us, "Since I work with children and babies, I use the skills I learned at home every day. I know what my kids did developmentally at that age, which helps me evaluate the children I care for. When I'm working with infants, I'm glad I'm a mother. I know how to handle and soothe them, and I feel real comfortable."

It's important not to feel defensive when applying for a new position. Clearly present the professional skills you can bring to a new employer. Don't apologize for having left the work force to raise your family. Instead, focus on your qualifications, as well as the extra experience you have gained through any community work you've done since you've been home. An employment counselor from Women Employed advised, "There's a critical turn in every interview. If you say that you stayed home because you made a commitment to raising your children, remember to say that now you're ready to make that same commitment to your career. That's what the employer wants to hear — that you do plan to take your job seriously after you return to work."

This employment specialist had another important piece of advice for women reentering the work force: use a functional résumé instead of a chronological one. (Most libraries have several books that can help you write your résumé. She particularly recommends *The Damn Good Resume Guide* by Yana Parker.) By organizing your résumé to list tasks performed and skills used, you can make a much better impression than by listing your work background chronologically. If you focus on the dates in your résumé, you'll only call attention to the time you were not employed. This also holds true for your education. If you leave off the date of your graduation from college or high school, you won't give employers the chance to figure out your age.

Some returning workers use a two-step strategy. They take a part-time or even temporary position to acquire a more recent work history, then use that history to help regain professional credentials. A transitional period of temporary and part-time work can help you and your family adjust more easily to the changes in schedule and

193

availability your new responsibilities will bring. Or, as we discuss in the next section, running your own business at home may better fit your personal employment goals.

Home-Based Businesses

Running a home-based business is one of the most popular options for women who want to resume paid work while maintaining an intimate connection with their children. It is estimated that 20 million households had income-producing home offices in 1991, up from 15 million households two years before.[7] In fact, close to 46 million Americans work at home at least part of the time.[8] A great deal of attention has been paid to this trend — you can go to your library and find dozens of titles on this topic.

Author Christine Davidson points out that making money at home is not a new idea:

> A woman making money at home is following an old tradition of American women. Women in both colonial and independent America ran boarding houses and inns; kept books for businesses; made and sold cheese and other foodstuffs; and assisted in operating farms, dairies, and various small businesses. . . . In finding the balance between caring for their families at home and providing income for their needs, it might be helpful for modern women to look beyond the conventional definition of traditional to what truly is traditional: a blending of home and work.[9]

Most home businesses are based on a woman's professional work skills. It is easier to build on what you've previously done in your career and apply those skills at home than to switch to an entirely new profession. One woman who runs a successful word processing service out of her garage previously worked as a legal secretary. After deciding to start her own business, she took some relevant courses on computers and telecomputing at her local community college. She and her husband then pooled their household savings and bought the equipment she needed for her business, including fax machines, modems, and computers. Her business is thriving. Many times she doesn't even meet her clients, instead conducting all her business with them electronically.

Other women find that a home business grows out of a hobby. Such businesswomen include caterers, seamstresses, and doll furniture or baby quilt makers. A *Wall Street Journal* article points out that craft shows have become big business and that a lot of money can be made at them, especially during the holiday season.[10]

Another idea is to focus on the needs in your community, as well as looking at your own interests. Day care is always in great demand and can pay very well if you look after several children. As a mother, you are already experienced in understanding and caring for young children, so this home business can build on your strengths as a parent. But full-time child care also can be exhausting, since you must juggle the needs of several children in addition to your own.

One idea is to offer before and after school care for school-age children. This type of service also is at a premium, as employed parents search for ways to find high-quality care for their children while they are at work. By becoming a part-time day-care provider, you can make some money and have playmates for your children but still have the bulk of your day to yourself.

Keep in mind that you generally must acquire certification to be a day-care provider. Contact your local and state government agencies for their regulations. Also remember that caring for a group of young children can be very hard work. When clients who depend on you come to your home daily on a set schedule, there is no such thing as a day off, catching up on your work at night or on the weekend, or a vacation.

The scope of possible businesses you can have at home is enormous. Here's a sample of the variety of at-home businesses the women in our survey have started:

- running a Christmas tree farm and nursery
- free-lance writing
- desktop publishing and graphic design services
- sewing custom "faux fur" coats

- typing legal documents and student term papers
- teaching flute or piano lessons
- bookkeeping and tax accounting
- selling Tupperware, Avon products, or Discovery toys
- testing software
- providing management consulting to small businesses
- providing home day care
- providing educational counseling and testing
- making baby quilts and doll house furniture
- booking author interviews for a public relations firm
- catering
- teaching Lamaze, parenting, or exercise classes
- maintaining computerized mailing lists
- preparing résumés
- doing custom calligraphy
- running a bed and breakfast

Despite the variety of home businesses mentioned, we've also found some common ground. Women who succeed in starting and maintaining their own home-based businesses generally feel a tremendous sense of accomplishment and satisfaction at contributing to the family income. But there are difficulties; working at home is not necessarily the best of both worlds, as many women believe it to be.

The most common problem is finding uninterrupted time to work at a home-based business. Many mothers have the fantasy that their children will play happily (and quietly) for hours at a time while they get their work done. This wishful thinking is often perpetuated by photographs in magazines showing a mother typing up a storm while her baby rests on her lap. This vision usually crumbles almost instantly when an important phone call with a potential client is interrupted by a toddler wailing in the background or the computer is put out of commission for several days by a glass of juice spilled over the keyboard. A child who feels ignored usually redoubles his attempts to get your attention, often by hitting his little brother or breaking one of your favorite china figurines. The reality is that it's just not possible to devote your full attention to caring for your children and to the work at hand. If you try to do both simultaneously, you may end up feeling that you're cheating both your customers and your children, and you will be frazzled to boot. It's wise to think carefully about the amount of work you can take on, scheduling considerations, and child-care options before you start a business.

Kathleen Christensen, director of the National Project on Home-Based Work and the mother of two daughters, believes that finding regular, dependable child care is essential to making a home-based business work.[11] This does not mean that you have to devote all your profits to hiring a baby-sitter, although many women do have a child-care provider come into their home to enable them to work. There are several other alternatives to consider. Don't overlook nap times and evenings. Most of the women we interviewed get all their work done during those times. It's remarkable how much can be accomplished in two to three hours per day when you are organized and productive.

Baby-sitting co-ops or shared child-care arrangements with another mother can free one or two days a week for your business without any money changing hands. Or you can wait until the weekend and entrust your children to your husband's care while you work in blissful solitude. As children enter preschool and school, you'll find many more hours a day to work. By setting aside a separate time to work without your children vying for your attention, you can enjoy the time you do spend with them without feeling guilty or pulled in two directions.

Christensen discussed other recurring issues of importance in an interview about her book *Women and Home-Based Work: The Unspoken Contract:*

> Talk shows and articles have presented the image that it's pretty easy — you buy a computer and you make a fortune. . . .
> There was nothing presented about . . . twelve-hour days, about having to work through the night, having to hire child-care help, or any of the middle steps that it takes to start a business: a marketing plan, dealing with clients, and just all the hours that it takes to make an at-home business go. . . .

[I found that] when a woman made the decision to have a job at home, whether or not it worked had a lot to do with the unspoken terms of her marriage. By that I mean what a woman's implicit expectations were of herself as mother, wife and wage earner. . . . I think the most essential [step] is the psychological boundary that says "I have work to do and I am justified in doing it." . . . It's only when women have that kind of clarity psychologically that they will be able to get what they need.

Those women who made [at-home] work work for them were very realistic about what they needed, and were able to negotiate in order to have those needs met. Since my study, women with at-home jobs have become more realistic. They know at-home work solves some problems, but that it also creates others.[12]

As Christensen indicates, it's crucial that you have family support for your business, since it will certainly cut into the time you have available for your family and for household tasks. Although your husband may be delighted to have you earning money again, he may not be so happy about pinch-hitting at home when your work load gets heavy, especially if the chores have been divided along traditional lines. It's a good idea to discuss this with him before you're in the middle of a time crunch and desperately need him to take his turn cooking dinner, doing the laundry, and putting the kids to bed. You should discuss this with your children, too. Preschoolers often have trouble understanding that even if you're home, you're not necessarily available to them all the time.

Time off is another problem. It's extremely difficult for a mother who does home-based work to find personal time. There is always something that needs to be done for her children, her house, or her business. If you're not careful, you may find yourself trying to fit a new superwoman ideal. It is possible to be busy every waking minute, and then wonder why you feel so rotten and unappreciated. *Ground rule number three: Validate yourself* applies here. Give yourself permission to get away from all your responsibilities and do something just for yourself. Make sure that you make time to visit friends, attend a play group, or meet with business clients or colleagues. Networking with other women who work out of their homes also can be helpful. If you barricade yourself in your home office all day and don't put some social interaction into your schedule, you can feel even more isolated than other at-home mothers.

Keep in mind also that you're unlikely to grow rich as a home business owner unless you work twenty hours a day. Many mothers take the long view with a home business. They start out small when their children are young and then devote more time and energy to the work when the children are in school. It can be tempting but dangerous to say yes to every assignment or work project that comes along. Caroline Hull, publisher of a newsletter for home-based mothers and mother of four children under the age of eight, warned, "If you only have twenty hours a week to devote to your business, don't take on work that will take fifty hours a week. You're setting yourself up for failure." By having realistic expectations of yourself and the amount of work you can handle comfortably, you will be more likely to be happy with what you're doing instead of feeling stressed and overwhelmed.

Home-based work is not for everyone. According to Kathleen Christensen, the main ingredients for success are a high tolerance for pressure and risk; love of being alone; negotiation skills with husbands, children, and employers; lack of interest in office routines and politics; feeling entitled to work; and a self-directed personality.[13] It also helps to be extremely well organized and self-disciplined and to be able to set priorities.

With these caveats in mind, you may find working at home a rewarding way to balance your own needs for professional achievement, intellectual fulfillment, and income with your need to be with your children. Newsletter publisher Hull believes that running a home-based business enables women to be "full-time mothers and part-time businesswomen."[14] She feels that operating a home business is one of the few ways mothers today can find the work/family flexibility they've been looking for. She has found that most mothers choose to work from home because they have control over their own schedules and can increase or decrease their work loads depending on their circumstances. A mother who works at home has the freedom to stop working when her child is sick, whereas a traditional employer would probably expect her to stay on the job.

Hull gives the following helpful hints for mothers who want to start a home business:

- DO be realistic — a home business will always take more TIME and MONEY than you think, so bear that in mind as you plan your business venture.
- DO do something you enjoy — it will be easier to be successful if you are working at something you truly feel enthusiastic about.
- DO check out local zoning ordinances and licensing requirements *before you start.* [These] vary tremendously from county to county.
- DO take yourself seriously as a businessperson — if you don't you can't expect others to.
- DO surround yourself with positive people — there will always be plenty of nay-sayers who will question your success potential. If you have the vision and really believe in it, give it a try.
- DO research — read everything you can on entrepreneurship, finance, marketing, home business.
- DO network — with others in home businesses, local Chamber of Commerce mixers, professional networking groups and associations, etc. Especially in the early days, networking with others can save you time and effort and help you avoid costly mistakes. Networking also enables you to promote your business via word of mouth.
- DO be flexible — your first idea may not be IT — be prepared to evolve and modify.
- DO be selective in your choice of a business enterprise to run from home. Accept your limitations and work around them by choosing a business in which *you* can set the hours and which will not require 60-hour-plus work weeks.

- DO be prepared for a period where your business is not making much money. Most new businesses take time to get established before becoming significant income generators.
- DO hook up with a mentor, if possible, and believe the advice she/he gives you. She's been where you are and is probably right!
- DO discuss your ideas with your spouse — his/her support will probably be essential to your success and will spare you agonizing negotiating sessions over issues crucial to your business.
- DO invest in some small business courses at your local community college. Most colleges offer excellent, bargain-priced courses on basic tax and accounting, business law, etc., as well as specific courses on setting up home-based business.[15]

A Home Business Success Story

Rita Anderson is a mother who turned a creative idea she developed at home into a successful, growing business. She is the founder of Partners in Play, a developmental play program for babies, toddlers, and preschoolers. She began her first program (originally named Leaps & Bounds) in Oak Park, Illinois, in 1979, when her oldest son was eighteen months old. Anderson now serves nearly 1,000 families a year at two suburban Chicago locations. She agreed to share her story with us.

"Because I have a background in remedial education, I devised ways of playing with my son at home to enable him to go through all the developmental stages at the opportune time," Rita said. "I structured the environment for learning, and we would play with the materials I made all day. I'd arrange our furniture as play materials — for example, the ironing board became a slide. When I went to pay my water bill one day, I ran into a man I had worked with during the summer at the Oak Park Recreation Department. I told him what I was doing at home, and he said, 'Wow, that would make a great class.' I went home and thought about it, and I decided that I'd try it, so my son would have other children to play with.

"I started with one class for young children, then added more as my son grew older. I started the infant class when I had another baby. My kids were in class with me when they were little. I wanted a business where I could be with them. My classes soon outgrew the city's playground — it couldn't accommodate the number of people who wanted to attend — so I decided it was time to go out on my own. This happened less than three years after I started the program.

"My family really helped me in my business. I couldn't buy the materials I wanted for my class — the right type of play equipment was simply not available commercially. My father-in-law, who had recently retired, said, 'Why don't we try making them?' We would argue out the details, he'd construct them, and I'd sand and paint. He also helped find the space I use for my classes. He found a church with a gymnasium that was rarely used. And my mother-in-law baby-sat my kids while I did all this work.

"I decided that the company would be not-for-profit, since I really wanted my classes to have an educational purpose. You have to decide what you're going to do. I didn't set out to make big bucks. I'm a person who wants to see kids grow and thrive, and a lot of that starts in infancy and toddlerhood.

"My advice to mothers who want to start their own business is this:

"1. Be prepared to do a lot of juggling. It does take some organization of your life. I still continue to have my kids as my number one priority even though they're in grade school and junior high. So I try to return phone calls in the morning. After three P.M., I want to focus on my kids.

"2. You have to be prepared to put the kids to bed and then work. That's when I get my typing and new lesson plans done. And I have to fit in my education. I subscribe to publications I need to keep up with in early childhood education. I carry them in a briefcase and read them if I'm waiting at the doctor's office or in the car if my husband is driving. I squeeze it in.

"3. Hire someone to do the detail work. I have someone come in to do registration and return phone calls.

"Success came more quickly than I thought it would. I also didn't expect this to be as time-consuming as it got to be. Currently, I'm cowriting a book about my program and activities that we're self-publishing. A woman who took one of my classes approached me about putting all my ideas in a book, and I thought, 'Why not?' You've got to risk something to get something. That's my philosophy."

As Rita Anderson's story illustrates, a business that you start at home when your children are small may turn into a thriving organization with several employees. Paul Edwards, coauthor of *Working from Home*, points out that homes are "the traditional incubators of new businesses."[16] Certainly, this is a growing trend for women who are dissatisfied with the options open to them in the work force. Women entrepreneurs are one of the fastest-growing sections of the economy. In fact, it is predicted that by the end of the 1990s at least 50 percent of American businesses will be owned by women.[17]

According to the *Wall Street Journal*, women entrepreneurs tend to be mothers with advanced degrees who have children three years old and younger at home.[18] Why not consider your own home-based business? As a graphics designer who has specialized in making baby products said happily, "I may not have to go back to work for someone else again!"

Where Do You Go for More Information?

BOOKS

Lynie Arden, *The Work-at-Home Sourcebook*, 7th ed. (Live Oak Publications, 1999)

Barbara Brabec, *Homemade Money*, 5th ed. (Betterway Publications, 1997)

Cheryl Demas, *The Work-at-Home Mom's Guide to Home Business* (Hazen Publishing Co., 2000)

Paul and Sarah Edwards, *The Best Home Businesses for the 21st Century* and *Working from Home*, 5th ed. (Jeremy P. Tarcher, 1999)

Liz Folger, *The Stay-at-Home Mom's Guide to Making Money from Home* (Prima Publishing, 2000)

Priscilla Y. Huff, 101 *Best Home-Based Businesses for Women*, 2nd ed. (Prima Publishing, 1998)

Looking Ahead: Taking the Next Step in Your Family Life Cycle

Loriann Hoff Oberlin, *Working at Home While the Kids Are There, Too* (Career Press, 1997)

Ellen H. Parlapiano and Patricia Cobe, *Mompreneurs: A Mother's Practical Step-by-Step Guide to Work-at-Home Success* (Perigee, 1996)

Lisa M. Roberts, *How to Raise a Family and a Career Under One Roof* (Book Haven Press, 1997)

Darcie Sanders and Martha M. Bullen, *Turn Your Talents into Profits* (Pocket Books, 1998)

PROFESSIONAL ASSOCIATIONS

American Association of Home-Based Businesses, P.O. Box 10023, Rockville,MD 20849. No phone number listed. Fax is (301) 963-7042. E-mail: aahbb@crosslink.net. Website: www.aahbb.org.

Entrepreneurial Parent, P.O. Box 320722, Fairfield, CT 06432; (203) 371-6212. E-mail: office@en-parent.com. Website: www.en-parent.com.

Home-Based Working Moms, P.O Box 500164, Austin, TX 78750; (512) 918-0670. E-mail: getinfo@hbwm.com. Website: www.hbwm.com. See Chapter 8 for expanded information on this organization.

Home Office Association of America, 133 East 58th Street, Ste. 711, New York, NY 10022; (212) 588-9097 or 800-809-4622. E-mail: hoaa@aol.com. Website: www.hoaa.com.

Mothers' Home Business Network, P.O. Box 423, East Meadow, NY 11554; (516) 997-7394. E-mail: communicate@mhbn.com. Website: www.homeworkingmom.com.

U.S. Small Business Administration, 409 3rd Street S.W., Washington, DC 20416; 800-827-5722. E-mail: answerdesk@sba.gov. Website: www.sba.gov.

WEBSITES

www.bizymoms.com
www.momsnetwork.com
www.wahm.com
www.workathomeclassifieds.com

www.entrepreneur.com
www.parentpreneurclub.com
www.work-at-home-dot.com

Options in the Workplace

Part-Time and Free-Lance Work

After running a home-based business, part-time work is by far the most popular choice for mothers who are reentering the work force. Since the late 1970s, the part-time portion of the work force has grown five times faster than the full-time segment,[19] and more than two-thirds of the 20 million part-time workers in the United States are women.[20]

In her research for *Sequencing*, Arlene Rossen Cardozo found that although 90 percent of the women she interviewed planned to resume their careers at some point, almost all of those women hoped to work part-time before returning to full-time work. She points out that part-time work enables a woman to "preserve her mothering priorities, working around her children's schedules, and it means that a career reemphasis is never a critical life change. Women who resume working part-time gradually integrate their work back into their lives so that their career commitments grow as their children grow."[21]

In our survey, under 2 percent of the women said they planned to return to full-time work, and more than 23 percent said they intended to start an at-home business or work part-time. Some women prefer part-time work because they don't want to be away from their children for eight to ten hours a day. Terri Choules, a mother of two preschool daughters, spoke for many mothers at home when she said, "I don't think I'm cut out for working forty hours a week, after experiencing the freedom of being at home full-time. Working from nine to two would be an ideal schedule. I want to be free when my daughters get home from school to give them snacks and to talk about their day."

Others like part-time work because it boosts their self-confidence. A woman we interviewed who works three evenings a week commented, "I feel my self-image is better when I'm working. I love to say that I'm a nurse as well as a mother. When I was at home all the time, I'd get really crabby with my husband because he was doing something that was important to him, and I needed a bit more."

Unfortunately, most corporations do not offer the type of professional part-time positions with benefits that most mothers (and many fathers) want. The want ads are filled with tempting career positions for which long hours in the office are part of the job requirements. Women who are eager for less restrictive work options often find that they have to create their own opportunities.

Persuading a former employer to customize a job position for you is often the most effective approach, since your employer knows you and values your work experience. Elizabeth M. Ours, a technical writer and at-home mother of three for four and a half years, found a great deal of success with this method. She told us, "Sometimes mothers have more options than they realize if they're willing to pursue them. When I couldn't bear to leave my daughter forty-plus hours per week but realized my husband wasn't ready for me to stay home, I began to search for alternatives.

"Although no one I knew had ever worked part-time at my company before, I asked my boss about it, and he created a part-time (three days a week) position for me. Soon after, other mothers converted to part-time. Not only did I help myself, but I paved the way for other women. Once I quit altogether, my boss provided me with a company computer at home, and I did editing, proofreading, pasting up, and small writing projects from home for the next two years. If you're not scared to ask, to be creative, or to try something new, you can often find employment that complements your mothering goals."

As Elizabeth found, telecommuting is a great way to work at home without having to spend a lot of time selling yourself and your services to new clients. Today many office jobs can be performed equally well at home by using the telephone and a home computer with a modem. Donna Malone negotiated a similar arrangement at the marketing research firm where she was a vice president. When her oldest daughter was two, she switched from working full-time to working three days a week.

She said, "My bosses were concerned about whether the area I was responsible for would still be profitable if I worked part-time. I wrote an action plan before I approached them, and we had several meetings about how we could make this work. I told them I'd be accessible on the two days a week I didn't work, and that it would be a good time for the person beneath me to take on more assignments. I took my job and dissected it, and I showed how I'd be able to handle the work even if I wasn't there five days a week."

This arrangement worked successfully for two years. Donna then switched to one day of work a week after her second daughter's first birthday. She occasionally goes into the office for meetings, but mostly she works at home with the computer and fax machine supplied by the company. She said, "This will only get better as my youngest child gets older and I'll be able to devote more time to my career again."

Women in other fields also have been able to set up flexible work arrangements. Nurses, in particular, are in such demand that they can set their own work hours. Other women work in a retail store or office during school hours so they won't spend too much time away from their children.

Karol Miller, an electroencephalogram (EEG) technologist at a medical clinic, is very happy with her part-time work arrangement. She works one night a week and every other Saturday. She has held this part-time position for four years, since her oldest daughter was eighteen months old. Karol told us, "This job gets me out of the house, keeps me current in my field, and gets me away from the kids at times. I was lucky to be able to arrange my own hours, so I only work when my husband is at home with our daughters.

"I think if I weren't doing this, I'd have a fear in the back of my mind: what will I do with myself when my children are away in school? I don't have that worry with this job. I'll probably increase my daytime hours when they both go to school. I think it's the perfect situation for me. I can still be home, but it makes me feel that I can do something else other than taking care of my children."

In looking for part-time work, you may find that joining a network of women can be a good way to discover flexible job opportunities in your profession. For example, Chicago Women in Publishing compiles a listing of members who offer free-lance writing, editing, marketing, and public relations services. The Association of Part-Time Professionals (APTP) is a national organization that promotes employment options for men and women interested in part-time professional positions. Connie Houston at the APTP says, "For ten years, we have tried to sell the idea of part-time work to employers, to make them realize it's coming, and that it's the wave of the future. People want and need time for their families, and part-time workers can do the amount of work that needs to be done, and in less time."[22] The APTP publishes a monthly newsletter for part-time workers that includes job listings. An annual membership is $20.

Working for a temporary service is another alternative for women who value flexibility. Temporary workers are in great demand because they offer employers an easy and inexpensive way to fill vacancies. More than a million workers are employed by temporary firms such as Manpower Inc. and Kelly Services, Inc., and 80 percent of those workers are women.

In 1989 *American Demographics* reported, "Much of the dramatic increase in temporary workers during the 1980s is the result of the increase in working mothers . . . who need flexible schedules while their children are young."[23] Many mothers work during the school year and then have the freedom to take the summer off. Most temporary jobs are in clerical and secretarial services, although there are also opportunities for engineers, computer programmers, accountants, health care workers, and others.

Of course, there are some drawbacks to part-time work. Employers usually pay low wages and do not provide any medical or insurance benefits to part-timers, let alone paid vacations. Participation in pension or 401K savings plans, as well as eligibility for company-sponsored education, also may be limited. Free-lance workers and consultants often face long dry spells between jobs. Part-time workers also have the problem of arranging child care and coping with limited opportunities for career advancement and colleagues who do not take them seriously.

Still, part-time work does give women an excellent way to keep their working skills up-to-date without having to resort to full-time child care. And free-lance or consulting work offers mothers the freedom to work when they want and to turn down jobs when they feel overloaded.

Job Sharing and Flextime

Other flexible work options include flextime and job sharing, which can be mixed blessings. Flextime is usually no help for mothers who don't want to work eight-hour days. Most of the companies that offer flextime enable parents to come in early or leave late, but they still work the same number of hours per week as other employees. Some employers enable flextimers to work four ten-hour days, which is more attractive to many parents. Job sharing can be a better alternative, but it's almost impossible to find. Most employers aren't convinced that two can work as well as one.

We interviewed Kim Meyer, a job sharer who has a two-year-old son. Her story shows both the advantages and disadvantages of this type of flexible work arrangement.

"Last year a major hotel chain offered me a position as office manager/administrative assistant," Kim told us. "When they first approached me about this position, it was a full-time, fifty hour-a-week job. I told them, 'I just can't go back to work full-time — I'm not ready.' A month later, they called me back and said, 'Would you consider job sharing this position?' I said, 'Sure!'

"In interviewing several applicants, they had found another woman they liked very much who would take the job but not full-time. She had a six-month-old baby at that time. It was the perfect arrangement for the two of us. She and I could decide who would work which hours as long as the job was covered five days a week. It was all up to us. We decided that I would work three days each week, and she would work two days.

"We also made a verbal agreement that the two of us would work as one person. By that I mean we agreed that the communication between Donna and me would be so good that our managers wouldn't have to relay information twice. We would each write a note at the end of our shift and then call each other at home in the evening if we had any questions. We only met twice in the six months we worked together. At first it was hard, but then we developed a comfortable routine. It was fortunate that our working styles were compatible, and we worked very well as a team.

"Our bosses liked the arrangement. On the days she was

sick, I showed up to work, and she covered for me when I couldn't make it. They also liked it because we were classified as part-timers, so they didn't have to pay any benefits. The only benefit we received was an unpaid two-week vacation, which we'd get after working there a year. They did pay us four dollars more per hour than their usual rate because they didn't have to pay for our insurance.

"We got a lot of positive reinforcement from the other women in the office. They would say, 'I hope they'll offer this to me when I'm ready to have a child.' Unfortunately, we got a new boss who didn't like this arrangement. It didn't fit with his managing style, and he didn't like seeing a new face there every other day. I just left this job because my husband and I are moving to another state, and my boss told me that they're no longer going to offer it as a job-sharing position. He actually told us, 'In the real world, you can't have your cake and eat it, too.'

"It's a shame, because it was an experiment. It was probably the first time that this company ever tried job sharing. A woman executive came up with this idea, and she hoped it would be a pattern for more people to follow. I would definitely recommend this arrangement to other women. It's a great way to gradually ease back into the work force after you've been at home."

One final option for parents who want to work but don't want to leave their children is to bring your child with you to the office. This option is rarely available, though, and there is no guarantee that your child will cooperate by sleeping peacefully most of the day. A fussy baby or an active toddler is not the best working partner. This arrangement works best in the short term, when a mother wants to continue nursing her infant or doesn't want to miss her child's first months of life. It also helps if you work in a small company and have an understanding employer and colleagues. It works best of all if you're self-employed.

A young attorney often takes his eighteen-month-old daughter to his office to play while he pounds the keyboard or talks to clients. He has done this since she was two months old. He works in his partner's comfortable home office, and both partners are usually dressed in blue jeans unless they have a court case that day. His daughter does fine in this setting, but she would not have been welcome if he worked in a large law firm.

While the majority of at-home mothers will probably return to full-time work at some stage of their lives, working on a flexible schedule — whether at home or for an outside employer — is by far the most family-friendly work option open to parents today.

Returning to Full-Time Work

Women who have spent years getting professional training or who are dedicated to their jobs are often eager to continue their full-time careers after the birth of a child. Others return full-time because of financial considerations or because they don't think they will be happy at home all day. They like having the challenge and satisfaction of doing work of their own.

Jennifer Hodge Jerzyk, a marketing services manager for a savings and loan, never doubted her decision to work full-time after her daughter turned eight months old. When we asked why she made that choice, she told us, "Because I find a lot of personal meaning in working. It makes me feel like an important person contributing to the world, and it makes me feel a lot better about myself. I came to the hard realization that I'm not very comfortable staying at home. I'm a project-oriented person, and I want to be accomplishing things all the time. At work I can find that kind of fulfillment. At home every day is much the same as the next. Though my daughter experienced a lot of milestones, there weren't any personal milestones for me. My husband and I also decided that from a financial perspective, we had less risk if we had two incomes, in case one of us lost our job. But the primary reason was that I wanted to continue my career."

Lucinda Michaelis, a speech pathologist who works in a Wisconsin school system, told us why she decided to return to work after a seven-month maternity leave. "I decided to go back full-time mostly because my job doesn't lend itself to part-time work or job sharing. And I definitely like the paycheck — being able to go out and buy a cute outfit for my son and not worry about it.

"It's also important to me that I have my own outside life that I'm involved in. I feel that when I'm with Andrew now, I'm a lot happier than when I was home full-time. I felt he was getting in the way of things I wanted to do. Now I'm so excited to see him at the end of the day, and I'm more willing to conform to his schedule. I'm not sure I'd feel that way if I worked part-time. I think I'd come home and say, 'OK, I have ten things I need to accomplish this afternoon,' and I'd resent it if I couldn't get them done.

"I'm lucky with my job. I have extended vacations at holidays and all summer off. I get home at four P.M. most days, so I have time to go out and play with him in the afternoon. My job works really well for our family situation. And I like the work I do. Working with children gives me a lot of ideas for caring for Andrew, too, which is nice."

Making the Transition from Home to Paid Work

When we asked mothers what helped them the most in making the transition from home to paid work, we received a nearly unanimous answer: the most important thing is finding a day-care provider you're happy and comfortable with. One woman said, "When I call home to see how things are going, I know my son's having a good day. There's a nice sense of comfort in knowing he's fine and he's not suffering any because I'm back at work." Other women said that they were most concerned with finding a good day-care provider in their home or close to their workplace and with making sure that their values and rules are consistently taught to their children.

While finding the right day care can be a source of anxiety, it also can be reassuring for mothers to know that their children are learning to interact with other children and are spending their days in a playful environment. One woman told us frankly, "Another advantage of having a baby-sitter is that she will do things with my daughter that I won't take the time to do — like going to the park every day or spending a lot of time playing with her. I feel she's getting the kind of activities that are important to her."

212

And, of course, there's always the joy of getting that regular paycheck and knowing you earned it.

In considering whether you want to return to a full-time or part-time position in the workplace, ask yourself these questions.

- What are my goals in returning to work?
- How much do I need to earn to come out ahead, once I deduct day-care, clothing, and commuting costs?
- How committed am I to advancing in my career?
- Would I be content with moving more slowly on the "mommy track" for a while?
- Does the professional status of a full-time career mean a lot to me?
- Can I accomplish what I want to at work if I don't work full-time?
- How does my family feel about this issue?

In finding the answers to these questions, you have to trust your instincts. Sometimes you just know when the right job opportunity comes along. Other times it can take months of soul-searching (as well as searching the want ads) before you find the work solution that is best for you, your husband, and your children. Whatever path you choose, keep in mind that it's not forever. You can always change your mind and your career path as your family grows and changes.

Conclusion

Whether you decide to stay home for a few months and then return to work full-time, or whether you opt to be a mother at home until your children are grown, we hope we've given you some practical help and a new perspective on making the most of your time at home. It's important to remember that *you're* in charge of shaping the role of at-home mother into one that fits your personality and your goals. If you use the four ground rules — determine exactly what you want your job to be, have confidence in your own skills, give yourself plenty of validation, and bring a feminist viewpoint to your life at home — to keep yourself balanced, you're most likely to find satisfaction and joy in your career as a mother.

When you look at all the years available to you and all the lives you can live in them, you'll be glad you opted for more, not less. Just remember, motherhood is a growth career.

At-Home Mothers Survey

We developed the questions in this survey after doing preliminary interviews with at-home mothers about their concerns and characteristics. Then, the survey was sent to over 600 women across the country, many of whom are members of FEMALE and Mothers at Home, the two dominant national associations for at-home mothers. We also conducted in-depth interviews with 40 additional women and men. These interviews, the 300 + completed surveys (many of which were accompanied by pages of additional personal commentary), and our own experience as women, professionals, and mothers, provide the research foundation for this book.

1. My decision to stay home was made:
   Before pregnancy   51.3%
   After pregnancy   15.7%
   After returning to work   11.7%
   During maternity leave   11.7%
   After birth of 2nd/3rd child   9.6%

2. My reasons to stay home were:
   We felt it was the best way to raise our
   child   26.5%
   Didn't want to miss our child's
   childhood   22.7%

Wanted to raise our child with our values   19.0%
Emotional attachment too strong to
leave child   18.3%
Other   5.9%
Work load too heavy   2.5%
Work schedule too inflexible   2.5%
Couldn't find adequate child care   2.1%
Can't afford adequate child care   0.6%

3. My husband's reaction to my decision
   was:
   Totally supportive   66.9%
   Worried about money   9.7%
   Somewhat supportive   6.4%
   Supportive if I later return to work   5.5%
   Other   4.7%
   Relieved   3.8%
   Jealous   2.5%
   Disapproving   0.4%

4. My friends' reaction to my decision was:
   Totally supportive   44.1%
   Somewhat supportive   35.2%
   Uncomprehending   7.0%
   Jealous   6.2%
   Other   5.3%
   Disapproving   2.2%

5. My colleagues' reaction to my decision
   was:
   Somewhat supportive   39.6%
   Totally supportive   20.7%
   Uncomprehending   14.9%
   Other   10.8%
   Jealous   8.1%
   Disapproving   5.9%

6. My family's reaction to my decision was:
   Totally supportive   70.4%
   Somewhat supportive   17.7%

Other	5.4%
Uncomprehending	3.0%
Disapproving	2.0%
Jealous	1.5%

7. The hardest thing about leaving my job
was:

Loss of professional identity/status	28.3%
Loss of income	24.9%
It wasn't hard at all	21.6%
Other	13.0%
Loss of friends	12.3%

8. My child-care assistance on a daily basis
is my:

Spouse	59.4%
Other	13.4%
None	11.9%
Preschool or mom's day out program	8.4%
Friend	3.0%
Other relative	1.5%
Housekeeper or nanny	1.0%
Neighbor	1.0%
YMCA or community center	0.5%
In-home day care	0.0%
Professional day-care center	0.0%

9. My occasional child-care assistance is
my:

Paid baby-sitter	22.5%
Other relative	17.0%
Friend	16.3%
Spouse	13.5%
Preschool or mom's day out program	11.7%
Neighbor	9.2%
Other	5.7%
YMCA or community center	1.4%
Housekeeper or nanny	1.4%
Private neighborhood nursery	0.7%
Professional day-care center	0.7%

10. Daily contacts with adults other than my
    spouse:

2–5	50.0%
One	19.9%
None	15.3%
5 or more	14.8%

11. My "time off" from child care in a typical
    work week:

1 evening	30.9%
1 morning or afternoon	20.7%
2–3 mornings or afternoons	16.6%
None	16.6%
2–3 evenings	8.8%
More than 3 evenings	2.3%
Other	1.8%
More than 3 mornings or afternoons	1.4%
1 whole day	0.9%
2 or more whole days	0.0%

12. My "time off" from child care in a typical
    weekend:

1 morning or afternoon	39.3%
None	36.4%
1 evening	17.0%
2 mornings or afternoons	5.8%
1 whole day	1.0%
2 evenings	0.5%

13. Things I do more of as an at-home
    mother:

Child care	11.0%
Cooking	10.8%
Laundry	10.0%
Shopping and errands	8.8%
Cleaning	8.7%
Reading/research	6.1%
Volunteer work	5.9%
Financial planning/paying bills	5.2%
Teaching	4.6%
Yard work	4.0%

Nursing	3.5%
Sewing	3.4%
At-home service or consulting business	3.4%
Hobbies	3.2%
Sports/exercise	3.0%
Sleep	1.7%
Household equipment maintenance	1.4%
PTA	1.3%
Sex	1.2%
Painting	1.2%
Going out	0.6%
Car maintenance	0.5%
Carpentry	0.4%
Plumbing	0.3%

14. Things I do less of as an at-home mother:

Going out	20.7%
Sleep	14.4%
Sports/exercise	12.6%
Sex	11.8%
Hobbies	9.2%
Reading/research	8.7%
Volunteer work	3.7%
Sewing	3.4%
Financial planning/paying bills	3.2%
Shopping and errands	2.9%
Cleaning	2.3%
Yard work	2.3%
Teaching	1.3%
Household equipment maintenance	0.8%
Car maintenance	0.8%
Painting	0.6%
Laundry	0.3%
Nursing	0.3%
Cooking	0.3%
At-home service or consulting business	0.3%
Plumbing	0.2%
Child care	0.0%
Carpentry	0.0%
PTA	0.0%

15. With me at home, my spouse does
    more:
Child care	11.9%
Yard work	7.6%
Household equipment maintenance	7.2%
Cleaning	6.9%
Shopping and errands	6.4%
Car maintenance	6.3%
Financial planning/paying bills	6.1%
Cooking	5.3%
Sports/exercise	4.9%
Plumbing	4.6%
Laundry	4.4%
Carpentry	4.1%
Sex	3.8%
PTA	3.8%
Sleep	3.0%
Reading/research	2.6%
Painting	2.5%
Hobbies	2.5%
Teaching	2.0%
At-home service or consulting business	2.0%
Volunteer work	0.8%
Going out	0.8%
Nursing	0.5%
Sewing	0.0%

16. With me at home, my spouse does
    less:
Cleaning	10.1%
Going out	11.7%
Cooking	10.2%
Shopping and errands	8.5%
Sex	7.7%
Sports/exercise	8.0%
Laundry	7.4%
Sleep	7.7%
Hobbies	5.3%
Yard work	3.2%
Financial planning/paying bills	4.8%

Child care	3.1%
Car maintenance	3.5%
Reading/research	2.9%
Painting	0.7%
Household equipment maintenance	1.2%
PTA	0.4%
Carpentry	1.0%
Nursing	0.4%
At-home service or consulting business	0.4%
Plumbing	0.3%
Volunteer work	0.9%
Teaching	0.3%
Sewing	0.1%

17. As an at-home mother, I would be in favor of:

Child-care tax credit for at-home parenting	13.5%
Larger child exemptions on taxes	10.2%
More home-based work	9.9%
Professional part-time work	8.9%
More flextime in business	8.7%
Job sharing	8.5%
National mothers' group to lobby government	8.3%
On-site day care centers	8.0%
Yearlong maternity leave	8.0%
National health insurance	6.1%
Yearlong paternity leave	5.7%
Year-round school	2.1%
Other	1.2%
National or state day care centers	1.0%

18. I belong to the following organizations:

Church/temple	24.1%
Mothers' group	14.1%
Play group	12.7%
Support group	11.0%
Other	8.3%
Schoolroom mother/aide	6.4%
Club or hobby group	5.1%

Charity group	4.9%
Library/hospital/museum/school board	4.5%
Professional association	4.0%
Community center	2.7%
Feminist group	1.4%
Local political organization	0.7%

19. Becoming an at-home mother has made my marriage:

Stronger	38.1%
No change	17.3%
Less tense	15.5%
Other	14.6%
More strained	14.6%

20. Its effect on my relationship with my mother:

Stronger	39.0%
No change	35.0%
Other	13.5%
More strained	7.5%
Less tense	5.0%

21. Its effect on my relationship with my child:

Stronger	50.0%
Less tense	25.7%
Other	15.7%
No change	7.2%
More strained	1.4%

22. Its effect on my own self-image:

More at peace	35.6%
Conflicted	27.1%
Stronger	23.9%
Lower	5.9%
Other	4.8%
No change	2.7%

23. My daily time in caring for my children is:

14 or more hours	42.2%

11–13 hours	35.1%
8–10 hours	15.1%
5–7 hours	5.4%
Under 5 hours	2.2%

24. Main source of positive feedback on
    my mothering job is:

My spouse	27.5%
Other friends	17.1%
My child	15.9%
My own parents	10.2%
Other	7.3%
Relatives	6.2%
Play-group members	5.9%
My child's teacher	4.5%
Neighbors	3.6%
I don't really have one	1.4%
Former colleagues	0.5%

25. Best aspects of being an at-home mother:

More involved with my child's development	14.3%
Not missing important moments	12.5%
My child is more secure/happy	12.4%
Satisfaction of being good at parenting	10.6%
Being my own boss	8.6%
More control of life	8.4%
Less stressed	6.7%
More time for personal interests	5.6%
Less guilt	5.4%
Getting involved in the community	5.2%
More time for my husband	4.7%
More time for friends	4.6%
Admiration of my peers	1.1%

26. Worst aspects of being an at-home
    mother:

Isolation	13.8%
Not enough money	12.9%
No time for myself	11.9%
Household chores	10.2%

Loss of identity and self-esteem	8.9%
Unable to accomplish anything	7.7%
No respect	7.5%
Less time for my spouse	5.7%
No financial independence	5.2%
Other	4.9%
Boredom	4.4%
Putting my career "on hold"	2.5%
Conflict with traditional roles	2.2%
Resentment of my husband	1.6%
Resent child	0.6%

27. In the future, I plan to:

Haven't decided yet; will see how it goes	15.0%
Become involved in volunteer work	14.3%
Go back for further education	13.6%
Start or continue my own at-home business or services	13.3%
Continue full-time mothering for more than 10 years	11.9%
Return to outside work part-time when youngest starts school	10.9%
Return to outside work only if it is financially necessary	7.0%
Embark on an entirely new career	7.0%
Other	5.3%
Return to outside work full-time when youngest starts school	1.2%
Return to outside work only if I can find acceptable child care	0.2%

28. My own mother stayed home:

Until her children started grade school	13.0%
Until her children entered high school	8.6%
Always worked part-time	7.0%
Always worked full-time	4.9%
Until her children graduated high school	4.3%
Had a business at her home	2.7%
Other	59.4%

29. If I had an opportunity to revise history:
    Yes! I would again choose to stay home
    with my children   97.8%
    No! I would choose to follow a career
    outside my home   1.1%
    Unsure   1.1%

30. I commented about life as an at-home
    mother:
    In the place provided for comments   62.6%
    In an attachment to the questionnaire   37.4%

A. You have my permission to quote me
   directly:
   Yes   94.5%
   No   5.5%

B. Character of my residential environment:
   Suburban   68.9%
   Rural   17.5%
   Urban   13.7%

C. Number and ages of my children:
   Total number of children reported by
   respondents   2.1
   Average age of the youngest child   2.4
   Average age of the oldest child   4.3

D. Duration of my role as an at-home
   mother:
   Average number of years as at-home
   mother   4.3

E. Highest educational degree obtained:
   Bachelor's degree   34.8%
   Master's or Doctorate   22.4%
   High school   15.4%
   Professional or technical certification   10.9%
   Associate degree   9.0%
   Postgraduate   7.5%

F. Last job title before at-home mothering:
Provided	91.5%
Not provided	8.5%

G. Household income before at-home mothering:
Under $20,000	4.4%
$20,000–$30,000	7.7%
$30,000–$40,000	13.3%
$40,000–$50,000	17.1%
$50,000–$60,000	11.6%
$60,000–$70,000	9.4%
$70,000–$80,000	12.2%
$80,000–$90,000	2.8%
$90,000–$100,000	1.7%
$100,000+	8.8%
Not provided	11.0%
Average income	$49,751

H. Household income after at-home mothering:
Under $20,000	8.2%
$20,000–$30,000	16.5%
$30,000–$40,000	22.5%
$40,000–$50,000	14.8%
$50,000–$60,000	11.0%
$60,000–$70,000	3.3%
$70,000–$80,000	5.5%
$80,000–$90,000	1.1%
$90,000–$100,000	1.6%
$100,000+	5.5%
Not provided	9.9%
Average income	$40,494
Average reduction in income with at-home mothering	($9,257)

I. Name:
Provided	86.6%
Not provided	13.4%

J. Age:

20–30	25.0%
30–40	67.2%
40+	7.8%
Average age	33

K. Location of residence:

Midwest	36.1%
Atlantic states	27.8%
Southeast	9.4%
California	8.9%
Southern states	4.4%
Southwest	4.4%
New England	3.3%
Pacific Northwest	3.3%
Mountain states	2.2%

Note: Percentages may add up to more or less than 100, since respondents could select more than one appropriate answer or could decline to answer.

Notes

INTRODUCTION

1. Mothers at Home, *Mothers Speak Out on Child Care* (Vienna, Va.: Mothers at Home, 1989), p. 5.
2. Michelle Osborn, "More Choose to Stay Home with Children," *USA Today*, May 10, 1991, p. B1.
3. Gail Schmoller, " '90s Choices: Balanced Life Preferred to 'Supersuccess,' " *Chicago Tribune*, September 8, 1991, Section 6, p. 1.
4. Gary L. Bauer, "Congress Gets the Child-Care Issue Wrong," *Wall Street Journal*, October 10, 1990, p. A18.
5. James Dobson and Gary L. Bauer, *Children at Risk* (Dallas: Word Publishing, 1990), p. 133.
6. The Gallup Poll News Service, June 4, 1990.
7. Bauer, "Congress," p. A18.
8. Ibid.
9. Dobson and Bauer, *Children at Risk*, p. 133.
10. Quoted in Leslie Baldacci, "The Homemaker — Then and Now," *Chicago Sun-Times*, March 14, 1989. Reprinted in *Sun-Times* special publication "At-Home Moms: Getting the Respect They Deserve," p. 8.

CHAPTER 1. MOTHERHOOD: THE ULTIMATE FULL-TIME JOB

1. Gail Susanne Corte, "Is At-Home Motherhood Enough?" *FEMALE Forum*, September 1989, p. 6.

Notes

2. Cynthia Copeland Lewis, *Mother's First Year: A Coping Guide for Recent and Prospective Mothers* (White Hall, Va.: Betterway Publications, 1989), p. 158.

3. ArLynn Leiber Presser, "Mom, a Sound Concept," *Chicago Tribune*, November 20, 1989, Section 1, p. 19.

4. Linda Burton, Janet Dittmer, and Cheri Loveless, *What's a Smart Woman Like You Doing at Home?* (Washington, D.C.: Acropolis Books, 1986), p. 74.

5. Mary Ann Cahill, *The Heart Has Its Own Reasons* (New York: New American Library, 1983), p. 2.

6. Quoted in ibid., p. 12.

7. Quoted in ibid., p. 299.

8. Thomas F. O'Boyle, "Fast-Track Kids Exhaust Their Parents," *Wall Street Journal*, August 7, 1991, p. B1.

9. Chris Golko, "Open Forum," *FEMALE Forum*, November 1991, p. 3.

10. Quoted in Leslie Baldacci, "I Control the Childhood My Kids Are Going to Have," *Chicago Sun-Times*, March 12, 1989. Reprinted in *Sun-Times* special publication "At-Home Moms: Getting the Respect They Deserve," p. 4.

11. Thomas E. Miller, LINK Resources Group in New York, National Work-at-Home Survey, 1987.

12. Terry Hekker, *Ever Since Adam and Eve* (New York: Morrow, 1979), p. 132.

13. David Ruben, "How Do You Spell Relief?" *Parenting*, February 1991, p. 98.

14. Quoted in Leslie Baldacci, "Group Offers 'Ego' Support," *Chicago Sun-Times*, March 12, 1989. Reprinted in *Sun-Times* special publication "At-Home Moms: Getting the Respect They Deserve," p. 2.

15. Arlene Rossen Cardozo, *Sequencing* (New York: Collier Books, Macmillan, 1986).

16. Janet Tavares, Letter, *Welcome Home*, June 1989, p. 27.

CHAPTER 2. MAKING THE DECISION

1. Elaine Badinter, *Mother Love: Myth and Reality* (New York: Macmillan, 1981).

2. Carol Miranda, "Keep the Spirit," *FEMALE Forum*, January 1989, pp. 4–5.

3. Arlie Hochschild, *The Second Shift* (New York: Viking Penguin, 1989).

4. Victor C. Larson, "Plan B," *FEMALE Forum*, December/January 1990–91, p. 11.

5. Lisa Napell, "The Stay-at-Home Option," *First for Women*, March 18, 1991, p. 84.

6. Chart created by Bruce A. Mahon, Glen Ellyn, Ill.

CHAPTER 3. THE FOUR GROUND RULES FOR YOUR LIFE AS AN
AT-HOME MOTHER

1. Anna Quindlen, "Mother's Choice," *Ms.*, February 1988, p. 55.

CHAPTER 4. MAKING THE TRANSITION

1. Loraine Goodenough, "Who Has *Whom* on a Schedule????" *Connexions,* Winter 1991, p. 3.
2. Beth Lindsmith, "Slob Story," *Parenting,* February 1991, p. 48.
3. Susan McDonald, Letter, *FEMALE Forum,* September 1990, p. 2.
4. Jan Kravitz, "On Decision Making," *FEMALE Forum,* February 1989, p. 6.
5. Quoted in Nina Barrett, *I Wish Someone Had Told Me* (New York: Simon & Schuster, 1990), p. 176.

CHAPTER 5. CREATING A NEW SELF-IMAGE

1. Jane Swigart, *The Myth of the Bad Mother: The Emotional Realities of Mothering* (New York: Doubleday, 1991), p. 49.
2. Anna Quindlen, "Mother's Choice," *Ms.*, February 1988, p. 57.
3. Quoted in Michael Minton, *What Is a Wife Worth?* (New York: Morrow, 1983).
4. Wanda Marie Block, "What Do You Mean, Go BACK to Work?" *FEMALE Forum,* November 1989, p. 6.
5. Deborah Fallows, *A Mother's Work* (Boston: Houghton Mifflin, 1985), p. 29.
6. Kenneth Labich, "Can Your Career Hurt Your Kids?" *Fortune,* May 20, 1991, pp. 38–44.
7. L. T. Sanford and M. E. Donovan, *Women and Self-Esteem* (New York: Viking Penguin, 1985).
8. Arlene Rossen Cardozo, *Sequencing* (New York: Collier Books, Macmillan, 1986), p. 120.
9. Sanford and Donovan, *Women and Self-Esteem.*
10. Adrienne Rich, *Of Woman Born: Motherhood as Experience and Institution,* 10th anniversary ed. (New York: Norton, 1986).

CHAPTER 6. PUTTING YOUR MARRIAGE ON A NEW FOOTING

1. Quoted in Ronnie Friedland and Carol Kort, eds., *The Mother's Book: Shared Experiences* (Boston: Houghton Mifflin, 1981), p. 28.
2. Janice Castro, "The Simple Life," *Time,* April 8, 1991, pp. 58–59.

3. Victor C. Larson, "Plan B," *FEMALE Forum*, December/January 1990–91, p. 11.
4. Quoted in Nancy Rubin, *The Mother Mirror* (New York: G.P. Putnam's Sons, 1984), pp. 28–29.
5. Claudia Bowe, "Money Matters," *New Woman*, August 1991, p. 110.
6. Arlie Hochschild, *The Second Shift* (New York: Viking Penguin, 1989).
7. Ruth Schwartz Cowan, *More Work for Mother: The Ironies of Household Technology* (New York: Basic Books, 1983).
8. Letty Cottin Pogrebin, *Family Politics* (New York: McGraw-Hill, 1983), p. 145.
9. Hochschild, *The Second Shift*, pp. 4–8.
10. Tracey Harrison, " 'Tyrant Children' of Working Wives," *Daily Mail*, December 28, 1990.
11. Christine Davidson, *Staying Home Instead* (Lexington, Mass.: Lexington Books, 1986), p. 27.
12. Linda Lewis Griffith, "Making Time," *FEMALE Forum*, July 1989, p. 7.
13. Becky Jonestrask, Letter, *FEMALE Forum*, May 1989, pp. 3–6.
14. Carin Rubenstein, "Is There Sex After Baby?" *Parenting*, March 1988. Reprinted in *Utne Reader*, September/October 1988, pp. 66–67.
15. Ibid.
16. Bruce Raskin and Bill Shapiro, "More Sex Please, We're Fathers," *Parenting*, March 1990, pp. 80–81.
17. Cindy Power, "Putting Sex Back into Your Marriage," *FEMALE Forum*, November 1991, p. 5.

CHAPTER 7. CHANGING RELATIONSHIPS WITH OTHERS

1. "Helpline," *FEMALE Forum*, November 1990, p. 5.
2. Alan L. Otten, "People Patterns," *Wall Street Journal*, November 28, 1989, p. B1.
3. Quoted in Ellen Creager, "Mommy Wars Pits Stay-Homes Against Employed," Knight-Ridder Newspapers, October 10, 1989.
4. Cynthia Copeland Lewis, *Mother's First Year: A Coping Guide for Recent and Prospective Mothers* (White Hall, Va.: Betterway Publications, 1989), pp. 11–12.

CHAPTER 8. PRIVATE NETWORKING: SUPPORT GROUPS

1. Rozanne Silverwood, Letter, *FEMALE Forum*, February 1990, p. 3.
2. Denise Lang, *The Phantom Spouse* (White Hall, Va.: Betterway Publications, 1990), pp. 100–103.

Notes

3. Much of the information in the resource list is adapted from the brochures and other materials sent by the organizations listed.

4. Quoted in Marlene Sweeney, "Thirty-Five Years Strong — The Same and Changing," *New Beginnings*, January–February 1991, p. 6.

CHAPTER 9. PUBLIC NETWORKING: INFLUENCING PUBLIC POLICY ON FAMILIES, WORK LIFE, AND CHILD CARE

1. Family and Work Institute, *Corporate Reference Guide to Work-Family Programs* (New York: Families and Work Institute, 1991). Quoted in "Family Issues Hit Home with Employers," *Chicago Tribune*, November 15, 1991, Section 1, p. 1.

2. Julie Solomon, "Schwartz of 'Mommy Track' Notoriety Prods Firms to Address Women's Needs," *Wall Street Journal*, September 11, 1989, p. A13A.

3. Carol Hymowitz, "Trading Fat Paychecks for Free Time," *Wall Street Journal*, August 5, 1991, p. B1.

4. Carol Kleiman, "More Men Are Bending to the Flextime Concept," *Chicago Tribune*, August 5, 1991, Section 4, p. 5.

5. Quoted in Hymowitz, "Trading Fat Paychecks," p. B1.

6. Sylvia Anne Hewlett, *A Lesser Life: The Myth of Women's Liberation in America* (New York: Morrow, 1986), p. 401.

7. Sue Shellenbarger, "Work & Family," *Wall Street Journal*, June 13, 1991, p. B1.

8. "Making Time for Families," from an editorial by the *Rocky Mountain News*. Reprinted in the *Chicago Tribune*, August 11, 1991, Section 4, p. 3.

9. While more research on families' basic needs is not necessary, researchers and family advocates do continue to come up with creative solutions worthy of note. For instance, Diane S. Farber, a mother of three and former social worker, wrote an article in the *Minneapolis Star Tribune* (January 7, 1987) titled "G.I. Bill for Parents." She proposed, "The bill would offer a stipend, if only an increased dependent exemption, while the caretaker stayed home with children. The caretaker who stayed home for a year or more would be eligible for career counseling, job training, higher-education benefits and job-search help." She went on to say, "We can look at parenthood as national service, and we can give women who are parents the same national support and sense of honor that we once gave men who were in the military."

10. Joyce Maynard, *Domestic Affairs* (New York: Times Books, 1987), p. 309.

11. Boston Women's Health Collective, *Ourselves and Our Children* (New York: Random House, 1978), pp. 211–212.

Notes

12. Anita Shreve, *Women Together, Women Alone* (New York: Viking Penguin, 1989), pp. 108–109.

CHAPTER 10. OPTIONS: COMMUNITY WORK, HOME-BASED
BUSINESSES, AND REENTERING THE OUTSIDE WORK FORCE

1. Arlene Rossen Cardozo, *Sequencing* (New York: Collier Books, Macmillan, 1986).
2. Penelope Leach, *Empathic Parenting,* Summer 1987. Reprinted in *Welcome Home,* November 1988, pp. 14–15.
3. Cardozo, *Sequencing,* pp. 178–184.
4. Quoted in Linda Chion-Kenney, "Another Way to Have It All," *Washington Post,* May 31, 1988.
5. Eleanor Berman, "Motherhood Is a Business Asset," *Family Circle,* February 21, 1989, p. 78.
6. Quoted in Jaclyn Fierman, "Do Women Manage Differently?" *Fortune,* December 17, 1990, p. 116.
7. Andrew Leckey, "Home Offices Fit Entrepreneur Era," *Chicago Tribune,* August 1, 1991, Section 3, p. 3.
8. Coralee Smith Kern, "Tracking the Home Office Worker," *The Kern Report,* January–February–March 1991, p. 1.
9. Christine Davidson, *Staying Home Instead* (Lexington, Mass.: Lexington Books, 1986), pp. 101, 137.
10. Dale Buss, "Christmas at the Craft Shows," *Wall Street Journal,* December 18, 1990, Section B.
11. Pamela Redmond Satran, "The No-Commute Career," *Child,* September 1990, p. 101.
12. Interviewed by Laurie Koblesky, "Women and Home-Based Work," *FEMALE Forum,* April 1990, p. 4.
13. Satran, "The No-Commute Career," p. 100.
14. Caroline Hull, " 'Womentrepreneurs' in the 90s," *Connexions,* Spring 1990, p. 1.
15. Ibid., p. 7.
16. Quoted in Margaret Ambry, "The Office," *American Demographics,* December 1988, p. 32.
17. Hull, " 'Womentrepreneurs,' " p. 1.
18. "Labor Letter," *Wall Street Journal,* September 26, 1989, p. A1.
19. Cynthia Copeland Lewis, *Mother's First Year: A Coping Guide for Recent and Prospective Mothers* (White Hall, Va.: Betterway Publications, 1989), p. 169.

234

20. Colleen Dudgeon, "Working Smart," *Chicago Tribune,* August 4, 1991, Section 6, p. 9.
21. Cardozo, *Sequencing,* pp. 189–190.
22. Quoted in Ellen Creager, "Mommy Wars Pits Stay-Homes Against Employed," Knight-Ridder Newspapers, October 10, 1989.
23. Nancy Ten Kate, "Here Today, Gone Tomorrow," *American Demographics,* December 1989, pp. 34–35.

235

Bibliography

Badinter, Elaine. *Mother Love: Myth and Reality.* New York: Macmillan, 1982.

Barrett, Nina *I Wish Someone Had Told Me.* New York: Simon & Schuster, 1990.

Baruch, Grace, et al. *Lifeprints: New Patterns of Love and Work for Today's Women.* New York: New American Library, 1985.

Baumbich, Charlene Ann. *Don't Miss Your Kids! (They'll be Gone Before You Know It).* Downers Grove, Ill.: InterVarsity Press, 1991.

Berk, S.F. *Women and Household Labor.* Beverly Hills, Calif.: Sage Publications, 1980.

Burch, Frances Wells. *Mothers Talking: Sharing the Secret.* New York: St. Martin's Press, 1986.

Burton, Linda, Janet Dittmer, and Cheri Loveless. *What's a Smart Woman Like You Doing at Home?* Washington, D.C.: Acropolis Books, 1986.

Cahill, Mary Ann. *The Heart Has Its Own Reasons: An Inspirational Resource Guide for Mothers Who Choose to Stay Home with Their Young Children.* New York: New American Library, 1983.

Cardozo, Arlene Rossen. *Sequencing: The Groundbreaking Book on Having It All but Not All at Once.* New York: Collier Books, Macmillan, 1986.

Chodorow, Nancy. *The Reproduction of Mothering.* Berkeley: University of California Press, 1980.

Christensen, Kathleen. *Women and Home-Based Work: The Unspoken Contract.* New York: Henry Holt, 1988.

Cook, Barbara Ensor. *A Mother's Choice: To Work or Not While Raising a Family.* White Hall, Va.: Betterway Publications, 1988.

237

Bibliography

Cowan, Ruth Schwartz. *More Work for Mother: The Ironies of Household Technology.* New York: Basic Books, 1983.

Davidson, Christine. *Staying Home Instead: How to Quit the Working Mom Rat Race and Survive Financially.* Lexington, Mass.: Lexington Books, 1986.

Dobson, James, and Gary L. Bauer. *Children at Risk: The Battle for the Hearts and Minds of Our Kids.* Dallas: Word Publishing, 1990.

Eagan, Andrea Boroff. *The Newborn Mother: Stages of Her Growth.* Boston: Little, Brown, 1985.

Ehrenreich, Barbara, and Diane English. *For Her Own Good.* Garden City, N.Y.: Anchor Press, 1978.

Eichenbaum, Luise, and Susie Orbach. *Between Women: Love, Envy and Competition in Women's Friendships.* New York: Viking Penguin, 1987.

Fallows, Deborah. *A Mother's Work.* Boston: Houghton Mifflin, 1985.

Faludi, Susan. *Backlash: The Undeclared War Against American Women.* New York: Crown, 1991.

Fraiberg, Selma. *Every Child's Birthright: In Defense of Mothering.* New York: Basic Books, 1977.

Friedland, Ronnie, and Carol Kort, eds. *The Mother's Book: Shared Experiences.* Boston: Houghton Mifflin, 1981.

Gallagher, Maggie. *Enemies of Eros: How the Sexual Revolution Is Killing Family, Marriage, and Sex and What We Can Do About It.* Chicago: Bonus Books, 1989.

Gordon, Suzanne. *Prisoners of Men's Dreams: Striking Out for a New Feminine Future.* Boston: Little, Brown, 1991.

Greer, Germaine. *Sex and Destiny.* New York: Harper & Row, 1984.

Harrison, Beppie. *The Shock of Motherhood: The Unexpected Challenge for the New Generation of Mothers.* New York: Charles Scribner's Sons, 1986.

Hekker, Terry. *Ever Since Adam and Eve: The Satisfactions of Housewifery and Motherhood in the Age of Do-Your-Own-Thing.* New York: Morrow, 1979.

Hewlett, Sylvia Anne. *A Lesser Life: The Myth of Women's Liberation in America.* New York: Morrow, 1986.

Hochschild, Arlie. *The Second Shift.* New York: Viking Penguin, 1989.

Kitzinger, S. *Women As Mothers.* New York: Random House, 1978.

Lang, Denise. *The Phantom Spouse.* White Hall, Va.: Betterway Publications, 1990.

Leach, Penelope. *Your Baby and Child: From Birth to Age 5.* New York: Knopf, 1989.

Lewis, Cynthia Copeland. *Mother's First Year: A Coping Guide for Recent and Prospective Mothers.* White Hall, Va.: Betterway Publications, 1989.

Lopata, Helen. *Occupation: Housewife*. New York: Oxford University Press, 1971.

Margolis, M. *Mothers and Such*. Berkeley: University of California Press, 1984.

Maynard, Joyce. *Domestic Affairs: Enduring the Pleasures of Motherhood and Family Life*. New York: Times Books, 1987.

Minton, Michael. *What Is a Wife Worth?* New York: Morrow, 1983.

Pogrebin, Letty Cottin. *Family Politics*. New York: McGraw-Hill, 1983.

Quindlen, Anna. *Living Out Loud: Home Thoughts from the Front Lines of Life*. New York: Random House, 1988.

Rich, Adrienne. *Of Woman Born: Motherhood as Experience and Institution*, 10th anniversary ed. New York: Norton, 1986.

Rubin, Nancy, *The Mother Mirror: How a Generation of Women Is Changing Motherhood in America*. New York: G.P. Putnam's Sons, 1984.

Salk, Lee. *What Every Child Would Like His Parents to Know*. New York: David McKay, 1972.

Saltzman, Amy. *Downshifting: Reinventing Success on a Slower Track*. New York: HarperCollins, 1991.

Sanford, L. T., and M. E. Donovan. *Women and Self-Esteem*. New York: Viking Penguin, 1985.

Siedel, Ruth. *On Her Own*. New York: Viking, 1990.

Swigart, Jane. *The Myth of the Bad Mother: The Emotional Realities of Mothering*. New York: Doubleday, 1991.

White, Burton L. *The First Three Years of Life*. Garden City, N.Y.: Prentice-Hall, 1985.